breath of the song

Jaki Shelton Green

NEW AND SELECTED POEMS

Carolina Wren Press
Durham, North Carolina

The mission of Carolina Wren Press is
to seek out, nurture and promote literary
work by new and underrepresented writers,
including women and writers of color.

Editor: Andrea Selch

Design: Lesley Landis Designs
Cover Image: "Lorelei" © 2005 Mark Rediske

Acknowledgments

"lifting veils" from *Poets for Peace*, © 2002 by Timothy F. Crowley, with
the permission of The Chapel Hill Press, Inc.

"a ransom of bones" appeared in *Immigration, Emigration, Diversity*,
(Chapel Hill Press, 2005) edited by Timothy F. Crowley and Jaki Shelton
Green.

Earlier versions of some of these poems appeared in *Hyperion, The Sun,
The African-American Review*, and *Black Poetry of the '80s from the Deep
South: Word Up* (Beans & Brown Rice, Atlanta, GA).

This publication was made possible in part by generous grants from
the North Carolina Arts Council. In addition, we gratefully acknowl-
edge the ongoing support made possible through gifts to the Durham
Arts Council's United Arts Fund.

Library of Congress Cataloguing-in-Publication Data

Green, Jaki Shelton, 1953–
Breath of the song : new and selected poems / Jaki Shelton Green.
p. cm.
ISBN 0-932112-49-8
I. Title.

PS3557.R3723B74 2005
811'.54--dc22

2005012707

I am extremely grateful to my editor, Andrea Selch, for her painstaking work, infinite patience, faith, and constant support which greatly facilitated the successful completion of this publication. I am indebted to David Kellogg and the entire Carolina Wren Press family for a legacy of encouragement and support. And thanks especially to Judy Hogan, who launched my publishing career.

Many thanks to the North Carolina Arts Council for the financial support that has made this publication possible and to Debbie McGill for her enthusiasm and encouragement.

My gratitude also belongs to my children, Imani, Segun, Eva, and to my beloved husband, Abdullateef, who passionately "knock from the inside."

And ultimately, my thanks to Allah, the whispering elders, my parents, and the spirits of my unborn lineages who caress my hands and dreams into words.

—JAKI SHELTON GREEN

There was a dawn

I remember when my soul

heard something from

your soul.

I drank water

from your spring

and felt the current

take me

—Rumi

for Abdullateef

CONTENTS

FROM *Dead on Arrival* 1971–1983

FROM *conjure blues* 1983–1996

FROM *singing a tree into dance* 1997–2003

NEW WORK *breath of the song* 2003–2005

Dead on Arrival

1971-1983

Purpose

i am new
poem
i am new
woman
writing
poems
about life
about thunder
and about
fading dreams
i am new
poem
real new poem
fragments of black juju tales
fragments of seaweed
and dust
i am new poem
skipping and flying
giving life
leaving no marks.

note to a dark girl

   i slip into black houses slip out of black slips black lace
black pearls and slip under your black fire burn into silvery
black rose buds slip into your skin and begin to sew up
black holes black hurt spots slip into black muscles and
realize that black bones hold up the mythical universe give
back black strength through black kisses and experience
black desert love experience unpoisoned black languages
unphotographed black breasts possessed by black babies
to listen and survive off black breath black discovery
heavy with black voices praying to black angels singing
black poems inside black nights black womb infused with
dark sperm nightmare black nightmare again black baby
black death black hunger black poems to fill the womb
black wind to guard against the rain black angels to cause
black salvation black springs black female child promising
life.

Eva I

the last Sunday
i remember you
in hat
pastels
soft gray hair posing beneath
your HATNESS
(only black women achieve the HAT-NESS)
that I envy you for.
You

> Grandmother
> African Methodist Episcopal
> Missionary
> Widowed minister's wife
> Mother of four
> grandmother of five
> great grandmother of fourteen
> HAT-NESS is inherited
> it's in the blood
> because I got the Hatness
> too –

>> i can put on your
>> old silk and taffeta and
>> linen dresses, petticoats and
>> suits – and top this little
>> head w/a panama
>> and hatness becomes herstorical
>> enriched w/Her/Your/Our style.

dust memoirs

I

candles drip air
washed away smiles linger to breathe;
a skeletal interpretation of motherhood
suspends itself above penurized nativity.
go into yourself and free those
midsummer visits free those grasshopper tragedies;
free those public telephones with passionate coffin smells
drip into your burial urn. drip.
this is called neurotic fiction. i am going out of myself into a
woman without skin, into a face without a mouth, into
a woman without a man i am woeman. woeman. this is
neurotic fission. drip, drip into my confusions. i am
vaguely alive, am dying alive native depression and
intellectual inclinations balance this head. keep it adrift.
i have no sweet songs of georgia pine to sing. i have no
succulent verse of carolina wind to whisper. i have only
come to bury my dead. i have only come to bury my dead.
this is my only sonnet. write in the dust with or without
the sandman's help…the moon is late. is somewhere raging
suicides and spreading apart skies. such is a product of my
unconsciousness. i do not know who i am and why i
choose…life? the writing will actualize the deed the
writing will fire the first plunge and sink the first little dove
into painless death.

II

it is the night that has decided to bring to me such taste.
such deafening shrills of roses awakening, even the earth
has danced around this bed, has whispered its wishes of
good luck. has called out to the sun to be obedient to its
lost father, to its wounded earthgod. kneel and receive.
it is the night that caresses the past and arouses its
haunting sport. doves of cocained misery fly into this bed,
offer gifts to this rich life root and kill themselves in the
shadow of day.

III

something still continues to open my head step inside and
dance with crooked swords. still as the black nights that has
recently decided to swallow birds and men whole that
stuffs the music of captivity inside my soul and compels
me to sing slave lyrics. a natural man of woe. woe man.
spitting dust into clean beds. spitting death into loose
lungs. playing broken keys inside sweaty seeds. sweaty
seeds about to germinate with bones. sticky bones grow
inside my lungs, pierce up through my head. blossom into
blood trees. blood seeds. coming down, coming out like
pieces of dead woman's tongue, burned white. alive.
with darkness. dead birds buried in fleshy rivers tear open
their thick bowels and balance each new clap of thunder.
bones and hearts and august sky burn together in celestial
bosoms.

Hips

Hips
Hips
Hips w/ bracelets of alligator teeth
python bells
hips undulated w/pheromone
hips w/african flavor
encasing your breath
your screams
hips laced w/wine
painted red blue browns
painted w/earth flesh
hips
choking your video fantasies
hips
black
brown
circles of hips
wading in the water
climbing mountains
hips
kneeling
praying
reaching
hips
nursing african civilizations
hips
enveloping
nations
black hips
sun baked
hips
planting
praying
aborting cancer
aborting ameriKKKa

hips swaying
under magnolia
limbs
hips
protecting
life
from
ropes
from
bullets
from poison
wombs
hips
sweet
round
strong
nation
hips
national
freedom
hips
hips
hips
these hips
painted
w/moon sweat
these full
virgin
hips
these
bridal
hips
carving
life before altars

these
mother
hips
these
hips
shaped
like
bowls
like
cups
like
vessels
these
pouring
spilling
swelling
authentic
natural
motherland
hips
hips
shaping
earth
into
babies
shaping
weeds
into
food
shaping
branches
into
knives

these
hips
aquiline
piercing
these
hips
of
purpose
hips
hips
hips
inherited
matriarchal
broad
like
breasts
hips
hips
with
crooked
eyes
seeing
sleeping
shifting
staring
hips
naked
w/silk
w/honey
w/cosmic nectar
w/virgin sweat

the moon is a rapist

why do you kneel there peeing in my window
you kneeling there upon my earth
impregnating the night crawlers with glow
their bodies do glow
as your soft yellowness penetrates my walls
you entered as you were
yellow streams of pee
leaving traces upon the bed
rapist you are
beating your rays into my buttocks
setting my breast aflame
moon babies i shall abort
moon babies come out of my birth pouch
soft rapist leaving me as the
sun knocks loudly upon my door.

night queen inheriting the silence of night

night queen inheriting the silence of night. the silence
of dead shadows pierce and break my dance. the room
becomes liquid. runs into my thick bones and i listen to
its echo. i listen to all the people i love, walk, embarrassed,
laugh at their thin frail emptiness. i feel lost and walk
through the streets like weather. i move my fingers over
his face and they burn, scorched with pain, truth. get rid
of your words lady, he once said. but i am myself. fill up
your mornings with afternoons. rip truth to shreds.

my mornings have become tinted with brutal motion.
brutal dance giving blood to the sunrise. i touch his face
again. this time it is satin. sweet. calm. but i have loved
all the people i can love. thin morning sweat covers my
skin. shivers my woman wetness. i don't want to sit
waiting for his poems to accuse me. i don't want to read
poetry, sing sonnets, dance with funk while my friends
die. to your question, i answered, no, i've never fucked
in spanish. i've never known midnight truth. this woman
wants to die. i will not smother her, i will give her back
to foreign men in unnamed cities who all chant her name
in seven different lingos. they already dig her grave and
harvest roses for her dark face. i will not smother into
the silence of her screams.

the foreign men sleep.
it is done.
it is done.
the lies creep up into you like the dust smooths itself
across the river. you light another cigarette. curse me
sharply in french.

if the walls were men, would they plot your death?
take off your face. the shadow is more beautiful. your
eyes have grown wings and flown away several times.
your lips become stone, shrinking innocent cries.

the musician hits notes at random. creates music
by accident. i again walk the streets like weather while black
notes form around my face. believe them, they are real.
they are thin, fragile, absorbing the whiteness of the sky.
remembering my face, remembering the foreign men.

they play a death melody. you are more beautiful than before he said. and i came again before disappearing into the dance, the weather, the foreign men. the foreign men disintegrating into my black skin. i remember each face before it died. before the breathing stopped. before the morning turned cold. i fasten their bones inside my mouth and write postcards to america's insanity. another man walked through me. creates pictures of foreign crying children. i scream hard and swallow him fast. i write more letters, this time to intelligent night spirits who will always remember.

and she died. and she died.

i have loved all the people i can. the poet. the musician. the full moon lady. the neruda prayer boys. the dying child inside me. i have loved all the people i can and you still come.

and you can still feel.

your wetness burns inside me. the rain smells funny. the rain smells like me. i continue pouring myself into you. you continue to drink cold color. i must write more. i walk to the window and curse the rain. they all sit robed in polyester disgust. they all sit with the taste of flesh inside their tongues. they sit. the white men and they wait. their polyester collapses and they are lost outside to full moons. fine black women eclipse their paths like birds, and the foreign men return, walk around them, suspended in slow motion. headless. they all come dressed in clean white warmup suits. the black angels present weapons and sink into thin pockets. before you kiss me see what you can see. your eyes. linked to the white suits. no, i've never fucked in spanish.

must people stare at his paintings. his poems, his dying woman. pull the curtains quick. there is a river giving birth inside. there is a moon. the father waiting impatiently.

to fear the beginning is much more. to fear my color is a pure act. a clean act. the foreign men clap and offer blind gifts.

i touch his face again. this time his paintings smile and
i take his dying seriously. you are emptying me again. i
am replaced by brown greasy bags and you eat all
the fingers inside. you eat all the fingers inside. your paintings
cry and your woman dies but the foreign men will not
come. they are afraid of the sun. they are afraid of the
egyptians. the warm light burns them. i am a pure image,
learning to fuck in spanish. learning to recognize your
pain. your smell has become the rain. thick with winter. i
want to touch her hair, but lower my hands again to your
face. burned again. you sleep during the day while i
choreograph funeral marches inside the bedroom. the
weeping foreigners sleep with you under your ugly
breath.
        i'll die on the street one morning with the sun pulling
apart my thighs, with the air peeling away my underwear.
i'll die beneath your polyester factories with the
nakedness of my breast turned east. beside a river with
old cars still smoking with anne's cough. her final cough.
beside the abandoned cement yard with old ovens wiping
sylvia's sweat from their doors. beside you with my
naked nymph shadow begging for forgiveness. neruda
designed simple dances for fresh girls in white muslin
to perform. i crawl into sylvia and wait. i am a perfect
river. swollen with myself. i die silently sandwiched
between winter and life. there are letters to write, prayers
to be danced. wet cement locks around me a winter wall.
i freeze like a perfect pencil. a sharp tip to be sliced off.
frozen. unable to keep the shadows out of my eyes.
unable to reach down to my female house. unable to
soothe my back and suck at my own nakedness. the
cement wall laughs and shatters itself into the darkness
of your eyes. the swallowed fingers rust inside your
stomach. your telephone rings. it is a telegram
from america.
        all your women are dead. your mother died inside the
smell of the foreign man. all your children laugh. come

back to your segregated bathroom at once. don't worry.
it is vogue, chic to hate foreigners. we'll wait for your
train. see you friday. love, the chains of peace.
      lady, forget your poems. lady, you always called me
lady. lady come feel my tall shadow.
      come drink life with me.
      lady, come dance under the moon with me. lady,
give up. leave sylvia alone. stop tickling anne. stop it
lady. lady if i laugh i'll cough up the fingers. lady,
there are seven foreign men at the door. lady, you fuck
so well in spanish.

Masks

i have worn masks
black
white
red
dead
alive
whispers
tears
i have worn masks
those come-here-baby-and-look-at-me MASKS
those
do-you-wanna-dance
Masks
those
PLEASE-DON'T-STOP MASKS
those Don't-Touch-Me MASKS
those catch-me-if-you-can
masks
those no-no-no
masks
those three-o'clock-i-can't-sleep-where-is-my-man MASKS
those-i-don't-want-to-go
masks
those please-please-please masks
those baby-i-been-good masks
those monday morning
smile-your-ass-off-please-be-kind-to-the-white-folk
Masks
those friday night empty
Masks
those torn masks
those hurt masks
i have worn masks
swollen full of history
masks
i have worn masks
crossing rivers
those please-hurt-me-
i-like-to-bleed masks

those half-white-birth
masks
those real masks
those brother-can-you-ever-
stop-playing-the-blues masks
those sunday-morning-
can-i-sing-can-i-choke-out-the-lord's-prayer masks.
i have worn masks
touched masks
face masks
tongue masks
those ape-like
rape-me-again masks
i have known new-england-
in-the-winter masks
ICE MASKS
sweat fire masks
i have known red
masks full of lip
poison full of sister-
kiss-me mask
MASKS I HAVE
WORN
hard, coarse, erect
Masks
masks
Masks. faces. western mask
behind obatala loveliness
i-know-faces. i-touch masks
i-touch-face.
i have known masks
masks screaming 'bout
being-late-for-my-own-
funeral
masks touching graves
unfolding tomb/wombs,
i have known chalk
masks. clown. stage.
sing-me-a-song

catch-me-again
do-it-again masks
i have known field masks
planting sowing
thirsting masks
known voo-do,
hoo-do-can-i-
git-you masks
wednesday-torn masks
sing-torn-melodies-
sing-fear-tunes-
wednesday masks
erasing saturday-
morning-full-of-
where-you-been-bitch-blues
i know masks
mother
daughter
sister
wife
masks
peeling
swallowing
leaking
sweating and
running masks
i-have-i-want-to-pain-
again masks
buried under
another man
another moon
another woman
mask.
got those
moon masks
full of numbers
full of ripe-time-to-be-
born masks.
i know masks

your masks
midnight i-want-
to-hold-your-name
masks
i know masks
your masks
full of wine
full of love
can-we-
compromise masks
endless
cosmic
poison
demon
MASKS
i have known
i have known
masks.
i have known masks
poet
dancer
music maker
baby maker
masks
full of breath
full of rhythm masks
meet-at-the-same-
time-same-place-
don't-be-late masks.
masks introducing
themselves at breakfast
masks unfolding-their-
wall-street-journal-into-
other masks. i have
known masks, rich-
college-boy-need-a-
piece-just-a-piece
masks.
i have known masks

fancy-colored-lady-
with-the-starched-
behind MASKS
i have known masks
bus stops
boat stops
plane stops
american docks
japanese motels
nigerian taxicabs
i have known masks
those $45-an-hour-
pour-your-masturbations-out
but-don't-cry masks
those silk-imported-
hand-embroidered-
natural-vegetable-dyed masks
those city masks
those purple-blue-i-want-to-
freak-you masks
i have worn masks
vegetarian
fruitarian
egoist
puritan
eating my masks
torn
worn
face masks
egyptian masks
female
feeding masks
i have worn masks
mother masks
daugher-can-i-teach-
you-now masks
morningtime masks
summertime-in-
carolina masks

baptismal
masks
election-time-
kiss-a-baby's-cheek
masks
i know masks
poet-lady
cry-baby-sitting-on-the-step masks
MASKS
MASKS
MASKS
MASKS
where-do-you-pack-your-
next-suicide
what-time-does-
the-hurt-stop masks
i know touch masks
i know fear masks
i know love masks
i know birth masks
i know old brothers
nodding on the corner masks
i know masks
your masks
train-plane-wherever-we-
meet-again masks
i know masks
savior masks
regenerative masks
i touch feel steal
masks
swallow
suck
vomit masks
rich masks
polyester-eat-your-progress-on-your-toast-
in-the-morning masks
memory
masks

old-songs-make-me-cry masks
new-lies-make-me-horny
masks
i know masks
grandma masks
mother-teach-me-the-meaning-of-struggle
masks
those six-o'clock-
see-yourself-murdered-
video masks
those camp-light-
pile-them-high-
burn-them-niggers
masks
masks
masks
masks
xmas time
gold light masks
sterling silver
mexican
inlaid american-coated
masks
i have known
masks
west coast
sierra
climb-your-ego's-ass-
break-fast
masks.
touch. see. whisper.
nature. season.
honey. butterfly.
seashore masks.
whisper from the ocean
full lady
moon masks
i know masks
abortion masks

aborted fears
tears smile masks
snapping beans
planting corn
waxing floors
masks
i know masks
geography
world politics
psychology II
education 234-but-niggers-register-w/english I-
prerequisite masks
quaker masks
cambodia. plant-a-tree-
earth-day-free-huey-can-i-wear-
an-afro-too masks
those sister
strawberry
café
fudge
au chocolat
sweet-talk masks
those jail-house-
visit-at-1:00 sunday
masks
those bed-time-
love-in-between masks
those masks between your
eyes undressing
my soul
touching-my-life masks.

All praise be the name

the tongues of this
womb voice
sing my mother's
birth song
sing her laboring cries
sing and cry
praises to her heavy breathing
creating self
this womb voice
melodic
wind caught
fire teased
so close to birth
so close to closing night
these tongues
teased by slavery
teased by freedom
teased by life air
these tongues
full of gold dust
casting
egyptian
womb tombs...
that an eager wind has blown
is not important
that a stormy tuesday night
sings
the blues too loudly
is my only testament
i sing into deaf cups
shower myself
among my own ghosts
as i collect
my aggressions
i understand the connection
the umbilicus
of my tears
to my blood.

Eva II

the lord is my shepherd
i shall not want...

does the shepherd have a wife
loving hands forming clouds
little creatures
centipedes and dust
loving hands forming rainbows
in grandchildren's eyes
does the shepherd have a soul-mate
earth rain in white hair
strength shining through a neon halo...a neon archer
the shepherd has a house
her pillars bronze aztec
centuries of egyptian snuff
in this golden vessel
consumed into this deposit of
civilization, this deposit in a shepherd land.

A birthday tribute I

my grandmother
Martin
probably/perhaps
was like your grandmother
bronze
high cheekbones
elongated
sculptured neck
pewter hair
an incredible carriage
always erect
poised
ready to succumb
eager to strike
eager to seek rest
peace
my grandmother
like
your grandmother
held your pride
your bleeding nose
your splintered chest
inside
her dirty apron pockets
held your head
your brains
under the heirloom quilt
wove
your words
your whispers
your prayers
into curtains
hung them high
my grandmother
like
your grandmother
would bathe in your tears
cleanse your wounds w/the milk of her nativity
cleanse your heart w/the honey of her offspring

grandmothers, Martin
knew how to do the do
to hold back the night
to stand in line when the line was a curve
with torches in the middle
grandmothers, Martin
bore your limbs
their teeth holding up your manhood
teeth mother
clenching tradition
and engulfing its shadow
you are the dream
of their stolen nights
the gardens
the cotton fields
the plowing
fresh
at the end of a weary day
you made the six mile walks over
snake strewn paths
to the white lady's house
to pick up dirty laundry
to seem necessary
take laundry back six miles
again
through forest
over bridges
dust
heat
wash
dry
starch
iron
fold
reload basket
carry it back again
you turned the fifty cents
into ethiopian treasure

you made the walk
a crusade
a carousing
a sweet tiredness
you gave them purpose
Martin
my grandmother/your grandmother
i know they were alike
sunday mornings
blue felt hats w/satin birds
ostrich feathers
they carried little red bibles
missionaries
quiet
humming
watching little boys like you
become men
become warriors
become statues
landmarks
historical footnotes
they were so alike
holding and sharing
the pain of granddaughters
losing sons, Martin
tears
letting go of the holy ghost
feasting at the love
table
early sunrise
prayer services
they link a great
circle
Martin
they climbed with you
we follow.

A birthday tribute II

                there were no poets there, none,
standing beside your crib
no firethrowers, no lights
but your mother knew
she felt this shango-child
that she had birthed
your fetal movements were
little echoes of boom, boom, boom
marching
little spears demanding
the wind to speak
there were no poets there
Martin
when you arrived but
your mother's birth pains
were sonnets
sonatas, lyrical, whispering
a far away drum rhythm
no poets
but your mother's blood
flowing
into your veins
your muscles
created another song
a loud freedom hymnal
and angels gathered in georgia too
winged you
birthed you
your memories of black faces
fire flies
clay dirt
mountains
your memories
trails of childhood
trails of history

no poets
from Selma to Montgomery
but your blood
always rhymed
no poets
hiding under dingy sheets
but their bullets
were fierce
alliteration
no poets
Martin
when you climbed the mountain
but when you echoed
we answered back
from the valley
as poets
in harmony
forceful
as only your poem of life could be.

A birthday tribute III

Martin
you are a master light
a black cat
jumping out of freedom's coffin
floating
crossing slavery's path
you are a master light
spirit glowing
spirit shouting
a master light
turning nights deep red
deep red
is the color of freedom
brilliant
burning
pulling the strings
of your own spiritual universe
you are deep red screams
loud
you are a man
who is loud
on the birth
of his ways
you redefine lives
souls
predict their worlds
your song is heard
your sun rays chime
your coming

A birthday tribute IV
the calling

your song-god awoke you from
slumber
your song-god
called you
put a cow's tail in your hand
asked you to sing
but you knew no songs
Martin,
but your song-god urged you
to sing for your grandfathers
and for your fathers and for
the sake of your house
and so, you did and from then and
until now
your mouth is
full of songs;
not good songs, not sweet
songs   not yet
then one day
the song-god returned
and this time,
he puts a horse's tail, a large, beautiful
shining horse's tail in your hand
a golden voice to sing
and you sing powerful songs
screams
blossoms
buds
fulfills young black seed
nourishes old black souls
freedom's coffin is sweet
no surprises
only smiling
stars
you are a
master light

spirit glowing
spirit shouting
spirit burning
songs that caused the dead
to come alive
songs that evoked the spirit
of the ancestors
i too shall be strong
and my voice
shall be
strong
my song-god!
my Martin
can you hear me
Martin
where are you?

Revelations

an old woman in me awakens patiently
i was born in 1829
late in the afternoon
the last red leaves were raping the trees
there was a full moon
the grannies in the cabins
kept a watchful eye on me
told me tales of how someday
truth
would set me free
free
in the elegance of african blood
blood sister
that knows the secret place
behind the heart
the secret place
beneath the veins
where the moon hides a dream
an old woman in me walks patiently
we evaporate into wind
smear blood over our thick
red lips
we smear blood under our african breasts
it is our baptism
our commitment
to each other's souls
from this day forth
we are locked in blood
blood sister
that knows the secret place behind the heart
the light shines through us
blood sisters
glorious red
glorious black

we are a cage of crystals
in the sun
our blackness
our africanness
more beautiful than the darkness
of imagination
i worship the light that pumps
your heart
i worship the dream you appear in
blood sister
old woman
tender
proud
fragments of myself
fragments of history...

Eva III

your thunderbolts follow us still
the old oak tree in the path
stands. still. its seams healed
now
we no longer use it as a clothes line
success requires a dryer
and never clothes hanging in the background
on sunday
ain't success a bitch
central harlem drive
haunts this granddaughter
where the poetess tries to create
sonatas with air
a hudson river angel repossessed
by these longfellow avenue
riverside drive skeletons
ah these thunderbolts
this prison-population explosion
this rain dripping blood
drowning our thunderbolts
our sunday morning smiles
your mission to deliver thunder
in small drinks.

for grandma

i heard your voice this morning
speaking from the foot of the bed
your quilt crawled to the
floor
as i lay down in the
first whisper of dawn.
i heard your voice this morning
the sound of cloth
a casual sound
a sunday morning
preparing to visit your lord
sound
half your life
half my life
half my daughter's life
we all dream of landscapes
romantic deserts
white sands
connecting us together
a half dozen roses
i play out my life
listening every morning
for your voice
at the foot of the bed.

Conjure Blues

1983–1996

praise song

you woman tree woman one
swaying to unheard of winds uninvented air streams
you woman sky with palms broad enough to hold egypt
who taught me to walk
slow and deliberate
like i had somewhere to go
who taught me stories
that needed telling
to love men and women who needed
who taught me to fetch life
out of the depths of rivers
taught me the words
that the tree branches sang to wake
the sun and bring morning home
who taught me to love loving
with my eyes wide open
who taught me to dance and smile
in rhythm
to clap with an open heart

i know the grandmother one had hands

i know the grandmother one had hands
but they were always in bowls
folding, pinching, rolling the dough
making the bread
i know the grandmother one had hands
but they were always under water
sifting rice
blueing clothes
starching lives
i know the grandmother one had hands
but they were always in the earth
planting seeds
removing weeds
growing knives
burying sons
i know the grandmother one had hands
but they were always under
the cloth
pushing it along
helping it birth into
skirt
dress
curtains to lock out
night
i know the grandmother one had hands
but they were always inside
the hair
parting
plaiting
twisting it into rainbows
i know the grandmother one had hands
but they were always inside
pockets
holding the knots

counting the twisted veins
holding onto herself
lest her hands disappear
into sky
i know the grandmother one had hands
but they were always inside the clouds
poking holes for the
rain to fall.

that boy from georgia is coming through here

they changed curtains
waxed floors
aired out the front company room
sent for camphor to lay throughout the house
they cooked all night
boiled bath water all day
cornbread, okra, turnip salad, stewed chicken,
fried chicken, dressing,
killed the prized hen
gravy, corn, potatoes, rice, sweet potato custard,
lemon pie, rice pudding, coconut cake,
chocolate cake, lemonade, and your chittlins,
martin,
all for you martin.
word was given sunday
that you was coming
to their corner
so they swept dirt yards
put the chickens up
hung out the special quilt
laid out the catalog sheets
put fresh oil in all the lamps
cause you never could tell
just how long you'd want to stay
a war on evil takes a lot of planning
takes a lot to get troops
stirred up.
so stewed corn with fatback, fried chicken
sliced tomatoes and cucumbers in vinegar
were passed around several times
soldiers need meat on their bones
martin
walking through dustbowls
hailstorms
riding on the blade
of a lightning rod
those old sisters
opened
their front rooms for you

opened preserves and jams
that had been put away
for something special
you were a something special
tall, brown, sweet with dreams
like their own sons
when they were about your age
before they drowned
in the dust
that you so gallantly
stepped lightly through
these were your first infantry, martin,
GRANDMOTHERS
whose words and dreams
shot straight bullets
these were your first line
GRANDMOTHERS
always ready to rinse out
a soul or two
these were the first line who put the armor
of sassafras, high john the conqueror, and
blood root
inside your shoes
made mountains continue to grow
in your daytime dreams.
yes, martin, songs
sung in kitchens
on front porches
in turnip patches
at hog-killings
carried the same verses
carried the same weapons
carried the same vision
in your name they gathered
washing, sharpening knives
polishing bullets
painting numbers
on their children's heads

gathering rain

i am a vessel
porous
waiting for your downpour
waiting for your
rain
to drench
swell within me

i am a basket
woven
intertwined
knotted
rewoven
waiting to be
filled
emptied
refilled

i am a cup
round
deep
oval
circular
waiting to be
filled
emptied
refilled
waiting to be
held
cupped

drink.

i am a box
flat
round
square
triangular

waiting to be
closed
hidden
filled
locked

i am your mystery
find me
close me
open me
await my
pouring
my opening
my closing

i am a woman
waiting.

eva/jaki/ivory/imani/eva

in the season of rising up in the morning
granddaughters give new meaning
to great day in the sky
sky with small fists
pinching clouds
reshaping stars
into skirts
wearing moon shadows like capes
we turn raindrops into buttons
stitch hair balls along the hems of
dresses
fire dresses
new granddaughters
wear new earth clothes
spell their name sistuh
prepare new warriors
to prepare new earths
check skirts for hems lined with hail dust
never admitting to treason

eclipses of eva

another mr john, mr otis, or mr tom
had died
i was six, first grade
smocked pink dresses from aunt cordelia
your big hand wrapped my small one
tight. gloved. like snow on sand
grandma why we coming to funerals?
that what good folks do
why they keep dying?
that's what you come here to do.
you tucked my plaits inside the collar
of the blue velvet coat
with matching hat
i hated this coat
you hated it too
but you agreed with mama that it was so
upper-class correct
that's what you wanted too
for me to always act like who we were
free black people
with free minds

but the blue velvet coat was everything
but free
a twelve-button prison without windows
without pockets waiting to be poked full of holes

aunt cordelia made me pretty dresses
plaids, corduroy, taffeta, dotted swiss
mama would brush my hair
and brush my hair
but curls would not leave.
you preferred braids.
you'd let me brush your hair
part it
grease it
plait it into one large basket
then we'd play "mommy"
you said your mama was always away

being a mommy to white children
when you were little
so i had to be the mommy
for you
that's when i liked you the most
i was a good mommy
i'd let you draw pictures
teach you to sew like you taught me
you always drew better pictures than mine
maybe you'd been practicing all those years
back when your mama was being a mommy
somewhere for someone else.

thunderstorms were best of all
you'd pull a chair
right up to the window and talk to god
for a long time
you'd be talking a mile a minute
real low, every once in a while i'd pick up a
word. nothing more
you could talk to the lord better than anybody
i'd ever known
he seemed to be talking back whenever you'd laugh,
closing your eyes, talking in hushed screams
then you'd sit and just rock
back and forth
back and forth
with your eyes closed
more words
racing like a train...

you prayed long prayers at night too
i never thought the Lord would hear you
in your teeny weeny whispering night voice
your prayer voice you called it
but i know better now

you eva tate's grandgirl ain't cha?
no, i'm mrs eva tate's granddaughter
you the one she used to take wit her
everywhere she went? how she doing?
my grandmother is fine. real fine. thank you.

tribute to the men and women who perished
in the imperial chicken plant fire in hamlet, north carolina
(a conversation i overheard in the fire)

there is still a sadness stuck in my mouth
that makes me wanna suck
on something that i have not tasted
for so long
what does it mean to not be able to remember
your mama's breast
bronze nipples, rising, falling,
but the blues remember
so without being able to explain
i feel this song surging inside of me
grinning, shouting
i feel this song my every question,
my why for, my how come,
my what did i do to be so black and blue
and it answers me by and by
in this new grave i choose
it answers like a moan.
no train came through those doors
no train whistle took us
out of there
no train crossing
red waters
no more welfare blues
no more politician blues
this morning has come
even down here
i got the same human hunger blues
and the blues hugged me back
as i watched my own hands
leave their prints on the fire's tongue
the blues hugged me back
when i closed eyes for the last time
and counted
mandingo
fulani
ashanti
ibo

counted all of us
before the fiery lynch rope
wrapped its tongue
around our throats.
the blues.
what else could i wail
what else would carry me
across yonder field of fire
not even the black of the bruise
could be called anything but red
i got the red fire blues
whatever we were as chicken workers,
never mind, whatever they tried to make us be,
no matter
our humanity
sang survival
we were white but the fire begat black
we were black and the fire begat black
together,
we became blue
blues people
and the blues bespoke our souls
in the church
my children sang strange words
to flat rhythms
they could not climb or ride on
king jesus was on the other side of hamlet
maybe he was checking birth certificates
driver's licenses, taxes
but he didn't bring no train
to bust through the door
i carry my past deep
inside these earth pockets
as my children sing flat notes
do they make love in heaven
are there brass beds
any music for people to party by

i guess it would take a blues man
to track me down up here
a blue black blues man
but not black like shackled nights or cotton
row black, or welfare line black
but JAZZ BLACK
blues black
soft black
any kind of song
can make a slave strong
but it's the BLUES SONG
describing to my baby
how my feet burned first
how my hands were broken in 38 places
how my hair became the sun
omega and alpha brilliant
a new shade of red
any kind of song
can make a slave strong
but it's the BLUES SONG
describing to my mama
that i tried to recall
the contours of her breast
the bronze nipple

imani

the first time your tiny lips searched for
my breast i knew that your soul had
decided to stay
grandma taught me babies were
spirits whispers wind souls cruising
through time sometimes they stayed
sometimes they roamed back into the
womb wanting needing to come again
knowing their birthing time
the first time i smelled you i knew
the earth flowers would be jealous
would feel diminished by your smell of
wind ocean sky
your taste was the taste of seed and
clouds and rain
your screams were the last thunderbolts
of my grandmother's woman tribe
we buried your veil beneath the
sage peppermint and blood root
i knew you would stay
you first dreamed of horses with no
heads who stood at your bed
laughing at you
their heads somewhere else
riding the night
you would talk to the moon
inside your crib
choreograph oriental operas
your tongue tasting herstory through woven quilts
of grandmothers past and grandmothers here
your cheeks sleeping on the
stitches of fear tiredness
happy stitches
strong stitches
patterned stitches of yourself
telling a life ready to happen.

for segun

nighttime
keeper of son moon-cradled tears
mother reaches inside knotted twisted boughs
tears flow upward back into eyes
with birthing shadows
not a time to be born
history repeats itself
grim reaper snatches
pacifiers of allurement
pacifiers of question
you curl beside your own lighthouse
your own beacon
your own guiding flash
into a nighttime that keeps you lately.

eva

numbers are a dance i danced
in the secret place
herbs are the jewels we
lost during the passage
new tongues burn unleavened bread
tongues spoken from the ears
are seen at night
and only precede midnight rainbows
we played the games of
rabbits
you taught me how to listen to the
quarrels between mr and mrs tree spirit
walk invisible through the meadow
thank you for the secrets between
white bread and magical nothingness
tasting like the first fruit
ah teacher of rhythm
and practice
and belief in demons of the light
who steal her soul in kodak wonder
thank you for muscadine hunts
thank you for the secrets
of strawberry and blackberry dew
and the difference between linen
and taffeta
easter and christmas
there are secrets tucked away inside
dresser drawers breathing quietly
your secrets line my dresser my closets
rhinestones feathers lace buttons
polka dot scarves patent leather
cashmere lambswool chenille
i found a piece of camphor beside my
pillow this morning
you the clever one who prayed
nightly who searched the woods of
your dreams searching for
womb roots to make more
secrets breathe

song of alice/ossie/nathaniel/ivory

i have drunk your bath water
rubbed the liniment of time
into crusting wounds
out of a windowless womb
you all climbed
out of my grandmother
named eva
you crawled
stood looking back up into vulva
up into her soul's crevice
standing on tiptoes holding
onto the womb's lid
you reach back up inside. wait for me.

i have loved all the people
i can love
the walls bleed back
your hands bloody
moist but alive
you slept as i crawled
down this mountain
you slept in her foothills
in her valley
you ate from her hair
waiting for me.

prayer for jesse

I

i will smear blood under your eyes
stand in the same dream with you
hear your secret screams
i will watch the light pump your heart
and worship whatever dream that swallows you
your silence will not protect you
for i have declared war
your speaking will cease
will be stopped
you will fear the visibility of my children's eyes
without which you cannot really live
we have declared a funny wartime
i stopped by your doorstep
stole your footprints
followed your shadow dropping
3 grains of sand from each print
i placed your footprints in the small
bags woven by african grandmothers
i will carry your footprints with me for 3 days
you and i will meet at the crossroads
i will toss your footprints in the direction
i want you to go
children play a funny kinda war

II

grandma used to say your mama
and your mama's mama didn't know nothing
about babies born with veils
for surely you were born with a veil
a veil that they did not bury properly in the
proper place at the proper time
grandma said you were such an evil white
boy because you'd seen the face of your own
devil
said if they'd buried that veil you woulda been
marching right up there on tv with dr king
instead of spitting on colored folks every night
after the news

grandma and miss gaynell said that the midwife
who delivered you musta put a curse on you
just because you chose to
come her way on that day

III
in your grandfather's barn
they found 12 white wax candles
        a bag of oranges
        several raw eggs
        a bloody towel
        2 ducks
        4 wingless pigeons
        7 fish
        a baby goat
they found all this spread on top of a bed
of chopped apples and oranges
facing east was a drawing of you
only your arms were birdlike
your hair dreadlocked
your skin like ash

IV
grandma said they shoulda buried that veil
but then white folks don't know no better
if i were you i'd find me some scorpion heads
9 needles and bake 'em in a cake
if i were you i'd dig in the earth and
claim me a veil
if i were you grandma said you should go
to the altar grind you up some
high john the conqueror and pray for rain

V
when i was a little girl all the grown folks around
me watched you every night
talked about you must be somebody's
necessary evil

you musta been somebody's mojo that had gone bad
these same old folks later sat on porches
rocked in the dark
hummed your name
stitching the sounds in the darkness with forked
needles
and even now from my grandmother's grave
she watches over you
saying lawd chile god sho' don't like ugly
she's singing sometimes
saying chile you oughta go to the altar
you oughta light you a broomstraw
you oughta find out where your mama hid
that first lock of hair she cut from your
baby scalp
grandma said you oughta go to the altar
oughta sprinkle some cast off evil incense
on the floormat of your car
grandma said you better read the 27th psalm
for 9 mornings in a row
yeah
you need to come by here
and listen to the slaves crying
and dance in their lynching light
you need to come by here and ask
for mercy

VI
your silence will not protect you for
we are a warring people
known for capturing truth
know to stop sentences in midair
your speaking will cease
you will fear the eyes of all children
you ought to get to the altar
and speak in tongues

for donald and segun

125th street market
beggars
choosers
priests unfinished unpainted
voodoo dolls for sale
       the priest sold cowrie shells
       his wife sold necklaces made
       from elephant hair
       they exchanged ivory for words
the city dresses up for mandela
winos reappear in the family album
needles fall from the arms
of alley squirrels
we run to take cover out of the rain

insult

bacon is burning again
overdue notices form a multicolored border
around the dresser mirror
his back is long, firm
rich redbrown like the glistening
tables he makes with his bare hands
it is a good back
bacon is smoking the kitchen
why does he not cook it in the oven
breakfast is in the yellow bedroom
he peels eggshells too hot boiled
she sits elbows at attention
sucking on mandarin orange slices
champagne boiled eggs oranges melba
he talks about the new woods from
brazil while the weatherman
comics the thunderstorms gaining
momentum in the south
it is a yellow bedroom
the egg yolk is running
splashes on his thigh
she wants to start there
licking the spill from his
hardness
only he'd push her aside and never understand
that she doesn't want to fuck
just enjoy breakfast

conjure blues

are you sure you want to travel this
red rope hair
blood locks
dripping history like a faucet
without gaskets
are you sure you want to travel
this path of kinky trails
interlaced with the breath of
ghanaian ghosts
this rope hair coarse this
rope hair full of tears this red
rope hair braiding little
splintered brains in alabama
binding arms back to torsos
in johannesburg
this rope hair wrapping
knives inside of babies' blankets
planting bullets under sunflower
beds
rope hair red rope hair
which wraps and unwraps your
nighttime fears your
white years of guilt
your nighttime tastes
of black lace, black woman
love
black braids unwrapping
unleashing unforgiving
red rope hair
are you sure you want to
travel this road
point to this cloud
wish upon this star
swinging from red rope hair
a lynching or a suicide

red rope hair strangling your truths
        my legacy our pain
        choking our offspring
        red rope hair a road
        crawl only no running
now i lay you
        down to sleep
        red rope hair stealing you at
        sunrise a sun crucifix a sun
        snake racing falling sleeping
        blood rope

i cry

it is my father's ashes glistening
on barren branches
the clouds were bloodstained
in the shadows
of ritual
called crossing
to name is to replace
to praise is to erase
to dance is to fall.
blood stains on red skin
need not be removed
from the lips of
children unnamed
or from the red crosses
in skies untouched
to touch is to smear
martin's voice was a piano key
this morning
out of tune
sharp
it is my father's ashes glistening
on barren branches
blood falling on earth
fertilizing the good
earth
dance martin
claim your own
cloud

auction block

open you legs gal
ain't gonna tell you no mo
now step right up you fine
virginia men of class
step right up and look at this here
gal's hole
now that's a well for a lot of drinking

aunt sue spread her legs wide
as six white men stepped forward to bid
on this hole
a hole that will soon suck them up into
its darkness
a darkness as wide as deep as her geography

aunt sue was bought by master peterson who
had a twitch for large african wenches
master peterson would visit aunt sue each
3rd full moon wednesday
she now knew how to predict his restlessness
her children by him continued to look
negroid
as if her body knew its own being
and refused to acknowledge his white seed
these children grew
disappearing before their mother's eyes
disappeared as a wedding present
to master peterson's sister down in
south carolina
disappeared when master peterson got drunk
in georgia and lost three slave boys
to a gambler
disappeared in exchange for a new set of

mules to the horse breeder in kentucky
third wednesdays
full moons
aunt sue gatherered nettleweed
saved strands of third wednesday hair
gathered blood from miz peterson's monthly
stitched out psalms using master peterson's hair
stood bone naked against the elm tree
of her father's lynching in midnight sounds
her womb gathering teeth from the rain

singing a tree into dance

1998~2003

rumors

what could the clouds be
whispering about me?
they don't even know my name

hush child!
hush

ain't i told you a thousand
times to whisper when we
walking thru the sky.

girl, cloud know your name
moon too
stars told 'em

they know 'bout you
know 'bout you before you were ever born

lifting veils

11 September 2001

I
it is a bloodstained horizon
whispering laa illaha il-allah
prelude to a balmy evening
that envelops our embrace
we stand reaching across
sands, waters, airs full of blood

in the flash of a distant storm
i see you standing on another shore
torn hijab
billowing towards an unnamed wind.

we both wear veils
blood stained
tear stained
enshrouding separate truths.

II
misty morning
teardrops of dust
choke and stain lips
that do not move
will not utter.
it is a morning of shores
sea shadows that caress memory
of another time
another veil
another woman needing
reaching
lifting

III
into your eyes i swam
searching for veils
to lift
to wrap
to pierce
dance with
veils that elude such mornings
veils that stain such lips
veils tearing like music

IV
it is the covering of spirit
not the body
my hijab your hijab
connecting interweaving crawling snaking binding
into a sky that will not bend.

bring me your breasts

bring me your breasts
the ones hidden
inside pockets
under geraniums
covered with babies' breath
bring me your breasts
the ones that exploded
inside a lover's mouth
pushing a millennium of light
down a pulsating throat
bring me your breasts
so that I might stitch them to
the morning rain and weave
scarves with the needles of
their nipples
bring me your breasts
the melon ones
the pinecone ones
the ones jiggling with memory
the ones crying with relief
bring me the ones you have buried
the ones you have
shaped into bowls, cups, razors
bullets
bring me your breasts so the
dolphins might carry them to the
center of the sea
the center of the waterfall
the center of the storm
bring me the breasts you wore to
the dance, the breasts wet with potter's clay
bring me your breasts
i will build an altar
a sanctuary, a garden
i will soothe and oil and massage
memory back into them
teach them to long
teach them to dance

teach them to remember their names
their reasons, their seasons

bring me the breasts
i am building torpedoes
for their ride to the moon
i am building bird nests for those
that will remain piecing fabric
to skin, skin to leaf, skin to
tree
woman tree totem
bring me your breasts
i need the needles from your nipples
i need the blood for your thread
i need skin for this house

bring me your breasts
the ones crouching in kitchen corners
the ones belching out the blues
the ones that have forgotten the names
of the tunes they whisper
bring me the new born nipples
the ones with teeth
the ones whose eyes forget to close

bring me the breasts
the ones waiting for eclipses
the ones who count full moons
and run off to count clouds
the ones that ache and re-stitch
themselves to your face
bring me the lynched ones and the choked ones
the strapped ones and
the pierced ones
bring me the left ones
and the right ones
the ripe ones and the ones
longing to ripen

bring me the curled ones
the arched ones
the ones that have become knives
slicing the air
bring me the ones you
bathe in ginger
and lavender
the ones you soak in
rain water

bring me your breasts
the ones that need
and the ones that are needed
the ones that are cold
and the ones too hot to touch
bring me the ones that howl at
the moon
and the ones that will not speak
and the ones that speak in tongues
bring me your breasts
the flat ones, the round ones,
the lump ones, the red, yellow
white, brown, and black ones
the ones stained and the
ones untouched
the ones photographed and
the ones uncovered
the ones veiled and the
ones drying in the wind
bring me the ones that are
awake and the ones too tired
to sleep
bring me the ones weeping
like willows and the ones
erect, sharp and full
of glass

bring me the silk ones
the linen ones
the cotton ones and
the wool ones
the ones bleached and the
ones unbleached
the breasts you wore to the
market and the breasts
you wore to church
i will build altars for these
sacrifices
i will build landscapes of your
healing

bring me your breasts
the mountains
the rivers
the paths
the gullies
bring me your geography
your rainforests and your sahara
i will navigate this map for you
with you, and because of you
i will strap this tornado of sinew,
muscle, bone, cartilage onto my
back and become the basket
so that you might heave,
stretch, and contract back into your map
your geography

bring me your breasts
the coconuts
tomatoes
papayas
pears
mangos
of your youth

i will replant the seeds
snip your flowers
and sing sunshine into
your veins, your roots

bring me your breasts
the ones that reject water
and will only root
inside fire

bring me your breasts
the celluloid, runway
breasts
the cleavage that outruns
the rest of your body
bring them to this altar
bring me virgin breasts
bring me the ones that sleep alone
and the ones that have
multiplied themselves in the
birthing of snow, ice,
glaciers
bring the ones that hold fire
and kneel before crucifixes
the ones who veil their eyes
and the ones that draw curtains at noon

bring me your breasts
your theatre, your opera, ballet, breasts
your breasts of crayons
papier-mâché
your breasts of wire
string and rope
bring me your breasts
i will wrap them in tinsel and
create anthems for their
stage

bring me your breasts
the large ones, amazon warrior,
dangerous weapon, signals,
codes, secrets
bring me the small ones
cupped, hidden, dangerous
weapon, warrior codes and secrets
bring me the ones that
drink seawater, the ones
that harden to the
smiles of children, men, women
alike
bring me the breasts that laugh
and the ones that cry
the ones that scream
and the ones that whisper
the ones that crawl and
the ones that run

bring me your breasts
i will place them at the altar
between sonnet and verse
between sways and bends
i will grow flowers
in their valleys and fertilize
them with honey

bring me your breasts
i will hold them to mothers
sisters daughters granddaughters
grandmothers aunts
cousins lovers friends
i will hold them in bowls
calabashes, baskets, hats
urns, boxes palms, wombs
cups, pockets, drawers, nets, bottles, tombs
skies, oceans

i will hold them in my mouth and hear them speak
of childhood girlhood womanhood motherhood loverhood
i will hold them in my womb so they might sprout
daughters sisters mothers to count the veins
we are holding these breasts in the captive light of morning
and the crystallized light of night
we become these breasts as we count ourselves back
into ourselves. our numbers our ages.
the weight of our tears
the height of our laughter
the width of our rebirthing

bring me the breasts
i will create a caravan
paint them
teach them the walk of the gypsy
the twirls of the dervish
the praises of the goddesses
the tricks of the shaman
the balance of the sky diver

bring me the breasts
i will teach them to moon walk
and teach them to write
we will write new songs
sitting on new moons
raising our skirts to the
crying mouths of a sky
that will not dry
i will keep the breasts near
and only touch them with
the feathers of the crow
only kiss them with the
lips of the crone

bring me your breasts
oh my mothers my sisters
my daughters my grandmothers
my lovers my friends

i will fold them and
help you tuck them
back inside, help you clear a field
and clean the ground for their
planting
bring me your breasts
the ones of amethyst, crystal, amber, and turquoise
i will soak them in my riverbeds
and dry them under the chinaberry tree
bring me your cedar, mahogany
and brazillan breasts your breasts of
teak and tortoise and marble and
clay
bring me your face, your feet
your hair and your nails
we will chase away the shadows as we
reinvent

bring me all your breasts
the ones with seeds, the ones with
bulbs, the ones with leaves, the
prickly ones, the sticky ones, the ones
growing weeds and the ones pruned and cultured
bring me the wild ones
the breasts that dress up in ribbons, purples, reds, velvet
and wear the smell of musk between their valleys
bring me the morning time
prayer time breasts, alongside the
peachy laced breasts of a saturday night fling
bring me your breasts
sisters of the circle
mothers of the yam
daughters of the shadows
bring them into the circles
bring them into the lodges
the houses the canoes the caves
the igloos the huts the holes the
attics the basements
bring them to me

bring them to your daughters
your mothers your granddaughters
your sisters
your aunts your grandmothers
your cousins your lovers your
friends

bring us the breasts so that
we might make ourselves over
and over again into the songs,
the dances, the poetry,
the stories, the jewelry, the masks,
the curtains of our new selves

i go into rooms with rumi

i wear new faces into rooms
i've never gone into before; faces
stitched by hands of grandmothers
whose skin is clay
whose clan is wind
awakening from earth's sleep

i wear new faces into a
pitch of circles
a sky of dervishes
a dance of holy

i sit with river tears
that have stained the throats of elders
burned the soles of
wandering infants
and laced the tea of thirsty virgins

i sit with the wide leaves of palm trees
leaves hurled from the recesses
of their color, their markings
i wear new faces into rooms
where i've never gone before

i wear new faces
crawling into southern veins
screaming veins
flowing into southern creeks
along side rail tracks choking with wisteria
tracks that refuse
to give back black bones
to black mothers
whose sons' skin is now the fabric of steel

we wash kinky babies in dew drops
gathered in secret
muscadine smells

send trails of rapture and salvation
into woods
full of hushed song
juneteenth hugging and dancing
reclaim bootlegging warriors
reclaim hootchie kootchie damsels
straightening their backs
while stretching their legs
clad with red fox
primrose pomade
starched mouths
rinsing out red clay stains
for a baptism that will not cleanse

who will be the messenger of this land

who will be the messenger of this land
count its veins
speak through the veins
translate the language of water
navigate the heels of lineage
who will carry this land in parcels
paper, linen, burlap
who will weep when it bleeds
and hardens
forgets to birth itself

who will be the messenger of this land
wrapping its stories carefully
in patois of creole, irish,
gullah, twe, tuscarora
stripping its trees for tea
and pleasure
who will help this land to
remember its birthdays, baptisms
weddings, funerals, its rituals
denials, disappointments,
and sacrifices

who will be the messengers
of this land
harvesting its truths
bearing unleavened bread
burying mutilated crops beneath
its breasts

who will remember
to unbury the unborn seeds
that arrived
in captivity
shackled, folded,
bent, layered in its
bowels

we are their messengers
with singing hoes
and dancing plows
with fingers that snap
beans, arms that
raise corn, feet that
cover the dew falling from
okra, beans, tomatoes

we are these messengers
whose ears alone choose
which spices
whose eyes alone name
basil, nutmeg, fennel, ginger,
cardamom, sassafras
whose tongues alone carry
hemlock, blood root, valerian,
damiana, st. john's wort
these roots that contain
its pleasures its languages its secrets

we are the messengers
new messengers
arriving as mutations of ourselves
we are these messengers
blue breath
red hands
singing a tree into dance

sonic collage/dying in a foreign country

i want to crawl into the grave
nibble along the wooden box
i want to nibble until my breath
becomes pinewood
i want to release you
into the cool smell of dark
touch your lips with my eyes
shudder when you awake

    i pour the wine
    sweep the ashes
    sift the wind's curse
    into bread loaves
    i pour the wine
    dry midnight tears
    stitch morning back into your eyes

        i pour the wine
        melt the glaciers forming in the fields
        scatter ashes
        rename daughters

daughters be the threshold of forbidden awakenings

i wrap my eyelids inside the feathers of day-old birds
i watch for the sprinkling of sun rain
winter grows inside my mouth

    thighs hips
        your hip bone
            connected to my...
                oh no...what bone

daughters dream fields of lavender
dream about whispering tornados
i be riding hip bones
sucking whale bones

shadows of beds chairs strangers
hurl through the cyclone

are we in morocco

i taste coriander
i am weeping egyptian licorice
these blues
these ambers
these saffrons
these curtains
these veils
these portals
these footsteps

are we in morocco

allah-hu akbar
i smell the prophet's blood
inside this windstorm
a saharan tease
a nile thirst

        you woman one
            river stone thief
                hostage to thunderstorms
                  ju ju rain
                        you woman tree
                          roots
                          boiling
                          blood
                          slave
                          carnage
                      you woman snake
                          licking
                          crevices
                          searching
                          indigo
                          flesh

```
            woman spirit
                  holding sky crumbs
                        stealing
                              chlorophyll
                                    from the night
```

I
woman sprout
woman dirt
woman flood
woman hair

II
wrap your woman stones
inside the feathers
of castrated cocks

III
wrap your woman honey
inside plantain leaves

IV
wrap your bones
inside the bear's coat

V
woman cloud
weeping flute songs
weeping flute dust

VI
wrap your woman child
inside tornados
lavender
bronze
tremor red

VII
hold onto your hair
hold onto your nails
hold onto your skin
your juice
your spirit dirt
hold onto your windows
your doors
hold onto your male children
i eat them
i paint them
i write them
i rename
redress
reposition them

VIII
i am ready
        i am the thursday night in brazil
               wednesday morning in monks corner
                   rehearsing
                        high priestess
                             litany
                 i am ready
                       red magic feet

                 i am bronze
          blue
                     female
                       ready

IX
i am the last morning
in the barn
sweeping
old dust
old memory
old worn out story
into worn out corners

                    i am skirts waiting to be danced
                         i am ready
                              i am veils
                                   ready to be lifted

X
i am the last night in the barn
candles
honey
penobscott fog
poems crawling from under the bed
poems falling off shelves
poems rolling from under rugs

were we in morocco

XI
i taste coriander
smell ginger in her hair

XII
poems lifted blankets, quilts, pillows
masquerading as sleep
poems spread open curtains
poems painted themselves on my lips
poems braided my hair
with the hands of my mother
poems oiled my feet
poems hennaed my thighs
poems crushed thunder chips
all over my lips
poems started licking my eyes
poems started caressing my face
poems measured my tears
that last night in the barn

XIII
in the barn
poems amputated your face
replaced your smell
your walk
your words

XIV
morocco is always here

i taste coriander
i smell ginger in your hair
my face is the shadow of all the poems
uncoiling
reaching
braiding
hip bone
to face

conjuring

I
bring me a crow's beak
four skins from four ribbon snakes
three day old robin's eggs
nine inches of black thread

eyes to blood filled cups
shoulder to parched lips
the angel drank all that your hands offered

II
soak your keys to the house
in rose water

i will not ever sleep again without your words
guarding my bed

III
soak his keys to the house
in camphor oil

your face aflame with birth
dropped seeds from pillow to pillow

IV
place all keys in a blue handkerchief

it is the light in the east calling my name

V
prick your third finger on your left hand

we stop sweating long enough
to remember to rename ourselves

VI
apply blood to four corners of blue handkerchief

earth angels disguise themselves as virgins

VII
fold
bury blue handkerchief
under his mother's doorstep

you present me earth for the flowers
for the midwifery of full moons
and seasonal eclipses

VIII
wash your feet before entering any room in your house

make me come on the edges of your poems

IX
plant violets inside his trumpet

i become ink
permanent inscription
on be-bop memory

X
cook rice before sunset

staccato of stains in motion
a color we could not name

XI
raise your naked feet to the ceiling

bruised melodies swallow a storm of fire
as earth angels grow wings

visitations

I
there is a lizard in my throat
it's been there since i was two
when i became thirty
and then for nine more years
it tried and tried to come out

only the clear oval eyeless fish
swimming on the bottom of my ocean floor
sing songs that convince
the lizard to wait
wait until she's fifty, she'll pull
the stopper
we'll all rush out

II
tonight is a time without sky
my son travels against dark light
i am convinced that a wiser
woman
an older woman with razors
inside her womb's gate
feeds him
ground snakes wasps nectar from
her breast

III
this is a living room formed
by my hands
i sit alone surrounded
by eucalyptus, benin masks,
masks with golden eyes, pictures
of all the ones who made
me who i am
pictures of all the ones who tell me my
name is granddaughter
plants whose leaves resemble
tongues, amber crystal, soapstone eggs,

shells that rattle with sea music,
turkish rings, kente cloth,
symbols of woman, daughter, mother
lover
symbols of funerals, weddings, gardens
symbols of daybreaks that look the
same as dusks

IV
there was a lover who watched the
lights change in my eyes
who counted my braids
mailed me pieces of the sun inside
envelopes that smelled like
cornfields, burned leaves
drying seaweed

V
there was a lover who used to
kiss my toes
tongue trailing the broadness
of my feet
before i painted them with
the sweat of hemlock

VI
there was a lover who swam
with the dolphins
snorkeled, presented me jewels
from the nile, from the waters
of the atlanta, from the creeks
of virginia
a lover who played music
backwards on the flutes belonging to
yemassee grandfathers

VII

there is a wiser woman
whose lips
hold my son until the night
rips back its covers

VIII

there are men i have loved
men i want to love
men i will never love
men i must love
men i cannot love
men i will love
men i will remember to forget
to love
but no man will make me smear honey
on his picture holding nine pins
between my eye sockets
no man will make me
present offerings to obatala
or cross my grandmother's grave
or wear white dresses for nine mornings
wear white beads, burn white candles
no more men will or can force me
to stand in the eye of firestorms
seducing the flames that lick at my
name

IX

no more men will i forget
their names or the names of their seed
no more men to cause me to speak
to the light in new languages that
singe the back of my tongue
no more men will cut slices
in my tongue as their gods will me to
speak through this woman house

no more men will open
the doors to my breasts
no more men will i count their footsteps
leaving my bed
no more men will i swim tired bloody
holding their weapons between my teeth
no more men will i give away to this venus
catcher inside my womb swallowing
their heads leaving me torsos
for my art

X
they will say
you are an angry bitch
they will say you are a woman
scorned
they will say
you need a good fucking
i will say damn straight
i am woman who is alive inside words
that turn silver at the edges
alive in a world of blues and whites
alive inside the head of the man
in her head
in her bed
alive in the living room having
left the man alone asleep
in her bed
she goes to write a poem
wait on her son listen to rain
kill an ant that's much too
black for the whiteness of her
curtains

XI
i will remember the other men whose
faces become borders for newly
painted other rooms other colors

breath of the song

2003-2005

wishing

razor blades did not

slash rainbows

hands did not

steal light from the dawn

prayers spoken in tongues did not

dissolve into silk pocket linings

air could be bartered

for fire

war could reinvent itself

as a prayer of silence

a ransom of bones

these bones
these bones
touch them gently
for their blackness
have been known
to pick
the locks of
hidden rooms
empty rooms
open doors

i have been this way before
passing as the *exotic foreigner*
denying the color of my
gloved hands
turning away from the dead
incantations of slaves
their voices rising
heaving through my throat
almost telling my secret

oh spirit
blow on me a slave wind
a night of stolen rapture
bleeding my name
from the river
where my blood is born

oh spirit
ritualize the collapse
of a black woman's sap
like the annual flow of the birch
interrupted by
a white man's decision

oh spirit
forgive me for the unfurling of
unfamiliar fabric

in unfamiliar rooms
that forbid morning to enter

i am the one locked away
the one paid for
in foreign currency
the currency of deceit

five hundred pesos a year

to change the water at
the altar

five hundred pesos a year

to remember to forget
a slave mother dying
crying veiled tears

my spirit returns
crossing dark slave thresholds
speaking through muted
smoke before collapsing
beneath my mother's fire

i have lost track of
my secret in this dance
i have lost track
of all other skin i've worn

the calculus of my sins
become sweet whispered drama
for the keepers of the secret

i have swallowed
all the keys
to all the doors
that keep me

oh spirit
touch these bones gently
when they appear
as screams
crossing borders
singing dirges
in familiar
tongues
revenge
sacrifice
i travel
to this myth of home
as transparent as faith
as transparent as the myth
of white face white neck
white arms white thighs
transparent as blue eyes

five hundred pesos a year

for the privilege to whisper
but these swallowed keys jingle
threaten to strangle me
with the story of betrayal
the story of a black girl
who walked through
the love light
of her mother's eyes
becoming
the story of a white woman
living on the edges of night

five hundred pesos a year
five hundred pesos a year

i pay my own skin
for the price of a key
a room a rape a birth

five hundred pesos a year
five hundred pesos a year
five hundred pesos a year

i pay
for this nourishment
this spicy soup of antebellum
i pay to commit these
sins of the tongue

to keep me white
alive locked away
in freedom's dusty
cubicle
locked away
inside someone else's journey

five hundred pesos a year

to anoint these bones
with the secrets
i weave to reseal
the lock
protect the unfurling
unfamiliar fabric of memory

five hundred pesos a year

to grow old
sit behind gloves
become
the bondsman's daughter
counting the tornadoes
i will unleash
painting my lips
with the colors
of somewhere else

oh spirit
bury these bones
under a forgiving sky
feed them the holiness of sunlight
the holiness of breath

five hundred pesos a year
five hundred pesos a year

to sharpen my nipples
their language memories
of another freedom
wait for the return of the bondsman

five hundred pesos a year

to lock away
what it is
he must never remember
the darkness of my body
offering up questions
he cannot answer
the darkness of words
that spill
all over floors stain chairs
eat into curtains
paint the walls
with the tongue of his seed

i joyously pay to write these other betrayals

to kiss memory
back into my bones

these bones
these bones
touch them gently
for they have been known
to dig themselves

into sky under skin
turn light into sharp crystals
walk across fire
turning this denial of blackness
into noose
tight intact
still within reach
breathing
disguised as river
needing
a new ransom

blistered joy
for rita

you enter our lives in
the roar of a purple faux
leopard coat
a lion's mane of dreadlocks
rock your face
for whatever smile
that remains unleashed
unmarried
free

you call
there is something
growing inside your brain

your laughter as bold
as your faux leopard signals

    not yet

we talk about your visit two weeks ago
thanksgiving day
you smile juicy words into the telephone
offering love gratitude longing for more
i tease you about sisters sweating your coat
we poetically
moan about bulging hips
jelly roll thighs

    not yet

reflect on grown daughters listening
to our outrageous stories
about hustling for the car payment
praying up money
to get to a writer's conference
living on sardines bagels apples
for the sake
of naming ourselves writers

already i am learning to miss you
your smile alone remains
unburied

we speak of rivers that
invent their own high tides
we speak of quilts
winter white sound

i must conjure mothers daughters grandmothers granddaughters
to help me stitch your shroud

we talk
about misbehaving characters
compare runaway manuscripts
to runaway relationships
i remind you
that i am hosting a celebration party
in honor
of your recent drama critics award

your laughter speaks to me in other tongues
other understood silences

we talk
in hushed whispers
about poems
that have offered
too much pain
comparing our poetry
to lovely sexual escapades
with lovers
too brutal to remember

your whispers tell me to gather oils, some soothing marvin gaye,
and a host of sisters

we speak
of crossing rivers

we speak
of the blood
that will not flow
and all the blood
that we've given

       we watch the moon now
            in the season of purple

we talk ourselves asleep
saying everything that needed to be said

       at the edge of your river
            we join you in a moonbath
                prepare for the washing of your feet
                   gather poetry for libations

i awaken to both your roar
and your whisper today
as shadows of leopards
and lions cross my
ceiling

       flow easy my sister
        flow easy

segregated rainbows

I
1932 somewhere
over the south carolina border
a yellow dress becomes canvas
witness to colorless dreams
that appear beneath
my grandmother's smile

standing together
under protective moonless starless sky
blond and black hair touching
daring the air
daring oceans between them

my grandparents clasp hands
stare into the invisible lens
of an invisible camera
they stare straight ahead into an erect future
cross burnings slashed tires backyard clothes-lines torched
dead cats hurled through windows

II
1953 i am born
granddaughter
the color of coral
ripened peaches
brown hair that rolls up into little rivers
i enter this world carrying
grandmother's birthmark
the same arrow pointing east
inside my/her left thigh

i grow my father's smile
when I cry
i grow the greystone wolf eyes of grandfather
when i am seven
my tears teach me
grandfather's language

III
i grow into the arrow inside my left thigh
i grow hair, breasts for the wind's daughter
i grow hips, teeth for the moon's wife

IV
i become the yellow dress
patched bloodstained hidden
i become the ground somewhere
over the south carolina border
receiving their dance their prayer
i become blond black hair bleeding together
i become their hands loving in and out of season
i become their land
fertilized by miscarried aborted ashes
i am the life
they could not birth
they could not name
nor not call home

V
my grandmother teaches me other languages
archery piano ballet
seduction rivalry
my mother teaches me to be her
not become the arrow
inside my left thigh
she demands that i cease walking
talking with wolves

VI
grandfather's obituary did not mention
my grandmother as his wife
my mother as his daughter
my uncle as his son
the wrinkled worn news clipping
chronicles and keeps the evidence of your memories
the smell of antique leather expensive cigars expensive smiles
collections of leather-bound books photo albums bank portfolios

new jazz brews inside of you
like chocolate wrapping licorice sticks

VII
i am the crying wolf
warrior without tribe
my ink well spills dust-coated ink
meant for a hidden canvas
moth-eaten
evicting shadows
of another likeness
another moth-eaten revenge

VIII
i become sword of the grandfather
become another trophy
memory persian rooms
satin afternoons tea biscuits
polite assassinations sexual innuendoes
piano recitals lullaby waltzes and proper chairs
i am the granddaughter
witness to the incest of rain and snow
witness to this betrayal of rainbows

IX
we bury yellow dresses deeds birth certificates
we bury swords teeth segregated deaths
we bury questions reprisals birth rights

X
every morning the wolf visits my yard
and i remember to feed him

measured regret

for my parents

I

i know you will not stand here long
i've measured your fear
its breadth
its depth
but it is hollow
therefore when you step back
name it guitar and
play another lullaby

II

you become a noose
though when i dressed
i called you scarf
purple turquoise heather scarlet
you wore me like sycamore
wearing black skin bark
you wore me loose

III

hair ransomed to wind
baby swallows seek new
warmth in december
december hair woven into
homes for baby birds
this noose their rapture

IV

what will my mother
my father
accuse me of now
starving
embellishing
imitating
forgetting
remembering
forgiving

V

my mother waited
for my father
to come home
from the hunt
it was all
a woman of eighty two
could do

VI

sixty two years
washing stitching
planting skin
on my father's back
sixty two years
digging
drilling for water
inside his chest
sixty two years
holding
cold dark hunger secrets

VII

my mother learned
to grow new hands new feet
dance with pulsating cloth
make silent the songs of rain

communion sunday

september 8, 1996

body of christ
body
body
body
body
body of body
body
body
blood of christ
blood of christ
blood of christ
blood of christ

i remember other
blood pouring
inside my legs
thighs in praise
blood of christ
at the communion table
i knelt in front of his righteousness

like kneeling before
drinking other wine
from his holiness

blood gushed from your lips
as your tongue probed my mouth
at the communion table
our eyes would not reach
across the blood of christ
the body of christ

my blood christening other communions

blood of christ
body of christ
make your humble confession
to almighty god
by meekly kneeling

i know it was the blood
i know it was the blood
i know it was the blood over me

at the communion table
i ate only the spider
that skipped
across the sacrifice

1

The Role of Congress

JAMES MADISON, principal drafter of the Constitution, held that in a representative democracy like ours, "the legislative authority necessarily predominates."[1] Take even a quick look at the powers given to Congress in the Constitution—passing the laws of the land, setting up and financing the departments of government, regulating commerce and trade, ratifying international treaties, raising and supporting our armed forces, declaring war—and it is very clear that our country's founders saw Congress as the foremost, dominant branch of our national government. They gave it most of the powers and had an impressive vision for what they clearly perceived as government's "First Branch."

On the other hand, many Americans today articulate a far less grand view of Congress, often not expressing much trust in it, rarely seeing it as a major factor in our nation's success. And a variety of sources—from administration officials to the media—will express or reinforce an executive-centered view of the government, with power drifting to the president, particularly when Congress doesn't live up to its responsibilities.

This chapter will try to sort this out—looking at the main roles and powers of Congress today, starting with why it really matters whether we have a Congress or not.

Why Congress Exists

I was once driving through southern Indiana on the way from one town meeting to another when I happened to turn on the radio. A commentator was attacking Congress. I don't remember exactly what we had done that annoyed him, but I do remember very clearly what he concluded. "We'd be a lot better off," he declared, "if we just did away with Congress!"

I remember thinking to myself how profoundly he misunderstood the U.S. Constitution and our system of representative democracy. "This fellow," I announced to the radio, "needs some lessons in American history."

You have to remember that the men who drew up our Constitution didn't want any single person to be able to impose his will on the country. They had just fought a war with England over that, and they didn't want to re-create anything like a monarchy on American soil. Just as important, they understood that even a leader who is elected by the people shouldn't be given too much power. That's why they divided the main powers of the federal government among the three branches. They believed freedom would be meaningless without a legislature independent of the president, able to represent the people of the United States in checking his desires.

Certainly the Congress has several important roles—to make the country work, to pass the budget, to manage conflict, to tackle the tough issues. Yet the most fundamental task of Congress is not to deal with any specific problem on the national agenda but to act as a check on the power of a single leader in order to maintain freedom for the American people. An independent legislature made up of representatives of the people is a key test of freedom in our country, or any country. Indeed, I doubt that freedom can exist—or ever has existed—in a nation without a free and independent parliament. So, ever since it was first set up as the First Branch in our system of government, the historic mission of Congress has been to maintain freedom.

If you visit the Capitol in Washington, look up as you approach the House of Representatives and you'll see, painted prominently above the entrance, Alexander Hamilton's statement, "Here, sir, the people govern." It is quite easy these days to proclaim cynically that Hamilton's words are just so much dust. Yet those who do are wrong, for Congress reflects us in all our strengths and all our weaknesses. It reflects our regional idiosyncrasies, our ethnic, religious, and racial diversity, our multitude of professions, and our shadings of opinion on everything from the value of war to the war over values. Congress is the government's most representative body. It is no accident that the founders gave it the power to make laws, to levy taxes, to decide how the government will spend its money, and to declare war. Congress gives the American people their voice in the counsels of power—or perhaps I should say "voices." By representing the multitude that we are, Congress is essentially charged with reconciling our many points of view on the great public policy issues of the day. That is why Congress often takes its time about things. To do their job, our representatives have to forge compromises, persuade others with the force of their arguments, and build a consensus behind an approach, if not a solution, to those issues.

I served in Congress long enough to know that it doesn't always do justice to all that the country's founders had in mind for it. But even when it doesn't serve a particular issue well, it still serves its larger purpose. "The numbers of men in all ages have preferred ease, slumber, and good cheer to liberty, when they have been in competition," John Adams wrote to his cousin, Samuel, in 1790. "We must not then depend alone upon the love of liberty in the soul of man for its preservation. Some political institutions must be prepared, to assist this love against its enemies."[2]

That is what Congress does—by acting as the people's voice against unchecked power, it is the guarantor of liberty. And for more than two hundred years, the American people have enjoyed a level of freedom only dreamt of in most other countries. That is why radio commentators who would wish it out of existence need to sit down, pick up an American history textbook, and think about it a little more.

Core Principle: Sovereignty of the People

Every summer, as the Fourth of July approaches, I'm struck by how inadequate a label "Independence Day" is. This certainly isn't to downplay the courage of our founders in declaring their independence from Great Britain or in fighting a war to guarantee it. But if you think about it, what we're really celebrating isn't a war; it's a concept. What was truly revolutionary about the American Revolution was the notion it enshrined that in a legitimate government, the people are sovereign, the ultimate rulers. Under this concept, neither Congress nor the president is supreme, because the ultimate authority lies with the people.

We take this idea for granted now, along with our system of representative democracy, because none of us has seen any other form of government in America, and because most other nations today—often following our example—are ruled by some sort of legislature chosen by the people. Yet at the time our system was being created, it was simply astonishing. To be sure, there were historical models dating to ancient Greece and Rome. But nothing was quite like what the framers devised, and certainly there were no models of such ambitious scope. The conventional wisdom of the day was that democracy on any but the smallest scale would quickly devolve into anarchy and mob rule.

"Again and again," historian Bernard Bailyn wrote about the founders, "they were warned of the folly of defying the received traditions, the sheer unlikelihood that they, obscure people on the outer borderlands of European civilization, knew better than the established authorities that ruled them; that they could successfully create something freer, ultimately more enduring than what was then known in the centers of metropolitan life."[3] The cry of "No taxation without representation" may have been born of frustration with dictates from the king of England, but it was rooted in the radical idea that people should have the final voice in their own governance.

The great phrases of the day ring through our history: "We the people," "consent of the governed," "blessings of liberty," "a more perfect union." These aren't just the technical terms of the scholars of political science. They are the words we live by, embodying the civic faith to which all Americans adhere. Our system rests squarely on the belief that freedom can only exist when one is governed with one's consent and with a voice in one's government. No one, the founders believed, is good enough to govern another person without his or her consent, and they embedded this concept in the bones of our system.

The question the framers had to grapple with, and one that remains a challenge for us today, was how to ensure that the people's views would be reflected in government. They recognized that a direct democracy—a system in which all citizens participate directly in making government decisions—had its limits. That might work for a small community whose citizens had the time and education to study their options before voting on how to proceed, but in a complex society it had severe drawbacks. Madison and his compatriots wanted to guard against the tyranny of the majority, to ensure that the passions of the moment could be cooled in deliberate debate, that the voice of the minority could be heard and its rights protected. And so they opted for a representative democracy, in which the people would choose elected representatives to carry their voices to Washington. This "representative assembly," John Adams wrote, "should be in miniature, an exact portrait of the people at large. It should think, feel, reason, and act like them."[4] Above all, it should be accountable to them.

This is, of course, the American experiment. No one knew whether dividing power among various branches and levels of government would ensure popular freedom and political ingenuity. No one knew whether, over the course of decades and then centuries, the two tyrannies feared by the founders—that of a strong executive, and that of a strong popular majority—could be constrained by a written constitution. And certainly no one knew whether Congress would, in fact, reflect the will of a teeming, diverse, and inventive society. At any given moment in our history, you could find Americans who would argue that the experiment was in danger of failing. Yet ours is now the oldest written constitution of a nation still in use, and its legitimacy remains solid. It has stood the test of time. But that does not guarantee it will stand all the tests of the future. We must never abandon our determination to make it a more perfect union.

Core Principle: Balancing Powers in Government

Some years ago I had the opportunity to spend several days in China with President Bill Clinton. At one of our stops, in a small community not far from Beijing, it fell upon me to explain the American system of government to a group of two or three hundred Chinese students. With only a few minutes to prepare, I did my best in the time I was allotted. The students were attentive and very polite, but I'm not sure I explained it as well as I should have. Indeed, I remember thinking to myself afterwards that I might have muffed a golden opportunity.

I have often thought about what I could have said to students from an entirely different culture to try to explain what the American system of government is all about. What is at the heart of our system that has allowed it to survive for so many years?

To me the key to understanding it is balance. The founders went to great lengths to balance institutions against each other—balancing powers among the three branches: Congress, the president, and the Supreme Court; between the House of Representatives and the Senate; between the federal government and the states; among states of different sizes and regions with different interests; between the powers of government and the rights of citizens, as spelled out in the Bill of Rights. The founders even discussed how the system they were creating could balance interest groups against one another.

The basic idea of balance is that no one part of government dominates the other. And it means that the decisions emerging from a process in which everyone has the right to participate are, in a sense, shared decisions, carrying with them a sense of authority and legitimacy.

Throughout the Constitution is an elaborate system of checks and balances to prevent abuse and concentration of power. Congress has the primary responsibility for passing the laws of the land, yet the president has the role of either signing them into law or vetoing them, and the courts can review whatever Congress passes. The president nominates judges to the Supreme Court, but the Senate must approve them. The president negotiates the treaties, but it is up to the Senate to ratify or reject them. The federal courts can declare laws passed by Congress and executive actions unconstitutional, yet it is Congress that creates and funds the federal courts, determines their jurisdiction, and has the power to remove judges. The president is in charge of the executive branch departments and agencies, yet Congress creates them, regularly monitors their activities, and provides their funding. And the list of shared responsibilities goes on.

The resulting system is a complicated maze of boxes and arrows on a flow chart that I would never expect my Chinese audience—or any other audience—to follow. But the underlying idea is a simple one: Our founders believed that the accumulation of power in any person or institution was dangerous and that balancing them off, one against the other, protected against tyranny. The challenge was to create a government that was powerful enough to act, but not with uncontrolled or unchecked power.

This balance of powers is one of the handful of core principles that has allowed our system of government to adapt to changing conditions over the past two hundred years. Rather than trying to devise a perfectly crafted, detailed system of government and setting it in stone, our founders provided the basic framework for our system of representative democracy with core principles like the balance of powers, the rule of law, majority rule (but with respect for minority rights), and making national laws "the supreme Law of the Land," under which there is flexibility for adjustment and change over the years. Thus, for example, the question of how the war-making power is balanced between the president and Congress is *still* being worked out, and in recent years the Supreme Court has rejected some Congress-passed methods of reviewing executive agency actions.

Yet the enduring principle that powers should be balanced in fundamental ways to ensure that no single part of government dominates and to protect against tyranny remains at the very heart of our system of government. This means that our system sometimes moves much more slowly than many of us might want. And it means that hearing from the many voices may sometimes lead to contentious debate. But to the founders, dispute and delay are simply part of the balanced system that prevents individuals or groups from imposing their will on the country.

The American people, despite their criticism of politics and politicians, have an unshakeable faith in the Constitution and in the American system of government and its power-sharing arrangements. The performance of government may disappoint them, but they firmly support the basic structure of our government set up by the founders. During all my years in Congress I never heard a constituent repudiating it. Americans believe that ours is the best system in the world and that it provides a framework for dealing with difficult policy issues while preserving our freedom. It may not be perfect or easy to explain, but it has served us well.

Key ways in which our system balances powers will be explored in the next two sections.

Congress and the President

Once a year, it's hard for Americans, ordinarily absorbed in their day-to-day activities, to avoid the news from Washington, as every television and radio network and every major newspaper covers the president's annual State of the Union address to a joint session of Congress.

On that night, all eyes are trained on the president as he outlines his priorities for the coming year. Members of the House and Senate from both parties applaud respectfully, sometimes enthusiastically. In this annual ritual of American democracy, the president tries to set a direction for the country, but in most speeches he also comes across as the nation's "chief legislator," giving the Congress its "to-do" list for the year.

It is important to remember, however, that the Constitution does not envision a master-and-servant relationship between the president and Congress. The framers of the document took care to create a system of government in which there is a balance of powers and extensive checks and balances between them. Indeed, the framers gave more specific powers to Congress, for they were wary that a too-powerful president would repeat the wrongs that the king of England had inflicted on the colonies. And they gave it a degree of independence from the executive that even today is rare among the world's major democracies.

One of my favorite remarks about the relationship between Congress and president came from former Speaker of the House Sam Rayburn. "I served with, not under, eight presidents," he often said. That probably sums up the sentiments of most members of Congress.

In our system, the president is entitled to propose legislation, but the Congress is equally entitled to dispose of it. His success at seeing his agenda enacted depends to a considerable degree on his skill at reaching out to legislators and persuading them to follow his lead. Because of the balance of powers, he cannot dictate to Congress what he wants, and he faces a huge task in communicating with

Congress because its very large number of members—535—hold many differing perspectives and represent diverse regional interests. The president often sees Congress as an obstacle to be overcome, and he always needs to calculate how his proposals will play out with Congress. One instrument of persuasion is the presidential veto, and sometimes with an overtly combative stance, a president can bend Congress to his will. But fostering a sense of cooperation and partnership with Congress—building coalitions of support—is typically the path to presidential success.

These days, we are accustomed to the notion of a president who is active across a broad front of legislative issues. But until the twentieth century, this was not the usual model of presidential behavior. Before then, more often than not, Congress was the driving force in American government.

In the nineteenth century, prominent congressmen such as Kentucky's Henry Clay were titans on the Washington stage for decades, while presidents came and went. For instance, when Indiana's William Henry Harrison was elected president in 1840, it was widely understood that he would look to Senator Clay for decisions on most important matters.

But in the first half of the twentieth century, presidents such as Theodore Roosevelt, Woodrow Wilson, and Franklin D. Roosevelt created the model of the expansive, activist modern presidency. To members of Congress, the president now looms large in the legislative process. He sets the national agenda and has behind him the vast knowledge and expertise of the federal bureaucracy. Using the "bully pulpit," the president can go over the heads of Congress and make his case directly to the American people. In this media-driven age, he speaks with one voice, rather than the 535 emanating from the halls of Congress, making it easier for him to command the attention of the cameras. The media seeks simplicity and vividness, and these are not qualities that Congress typically displays.

The relationship between Congress and the president is central to the workings of our system of government, and tension and struggle between these two rivals for power is inevitable under our Constitution. The framers did not set out to promote gridlock between them, but they did want to balance one off against the other and make sure that conflicting opinions in society should be considered carefully before government acts.

Ours is clearly not a system set up for quick, efficient action, and sorting out who has the real power between the president and Congress on a host of matters is not easy. But more often than not, Congresses and presidents find a way to work with each other, cooperating where possible, and the nation's business gets done. Their relationship, while at times tumultuous, in the end safeguards the people from corruption of power and abuse of authority—by either side. It is a system that works—not perfectly, to be sure, but certainly more than adequately.

Why Federalism Works

Early in my congressional career, I discovered a simple truth about our governmental system: It's confusing. Like most new members of Congress, I had taken office with visions of wrestling with the future of our Republic. So it came as something of a shock to learn that much of what my constituents wanted from me was help in navigating the federal, state, and local bureaucracies.

If you think back to your seventh-grade civics class, you'll remember learning about a system that resembles a layer cake, with local government at the bottom, the states in the middle, and the federal government at the top, all clearly delineated. That's still how most of us think of "federalism," or the division of responsibilities among different levels of government. But we're hopelessly out of date. If anything, the American political system is like a marble cake, with a blend of elected and appointed officials from all levels of government sharing policy and program duties.

Think about transportation, for instance. It's difficult enough to figure out which agency at which level of government maintains a particular stretch of roadway. But it can be next to impossible to untangle how a given decision was made about putting it there in the first place. The funding was provided by Congress, as were certain guidelines on how the money could be spent, but the specifics were up to a welter of state, county, and local elected officials and highway engineers. You can find the same assortment of responsibilities in everything from the administration of welfare benefits to law enforcement to cleaning up toxic waste.

There's a reason for this. As with many of the questions we sort through as a nation, the basic framework for dividing governmental responsibilities was set by the Constitution. Although the founders were quite specific on some matters—states, for instance, don't have the power to declare war or coin money—they deliberately left much room for flexibility. Just as they believed that dividing power among the various branches of the federal government would make it more responsive, so would dividing power among the different levels. "[It] is not by the consolidation, or concentration of powers, but by their distribution, that good government is effected," Thomas Jefferson wrote. "Were not this great country already divided into states, that division must be made, that each might do for itself what concerns itself directly, and what it can so much better do than a distant authority. . . . Were we directed from Washington when to sow, and when to reap, we should soon want bread."[5]

And so, over the decades, each level of government has seen its share of responsibilities ebb and flow with the demands of the era. The New Deal, for instance, brought new power to Washington, with its myriad of federal agencies helping American individuals and communities cope with the aftermath of the Depression; so, too, did the civil rights movement, which relied on federal authority to bring about change in the states. On the other hand, over the last two decades a mix of federal cutbacks, legislative changes, and Supreme Court decisions have returned authority to the states and even local communities. In some cases, this has been driven by an ideological belief that problems should be resolved closer to where people actually live, rather than by federal power. In other cases, it has been driven by practicality, as new approaches to problems bubble up from the states—as was the case with welfare reform.

We live in an era that is more difficult to categorize. On the one hand, the federal government has responded to the threat of terrorism by expanding and consolidating its power, especially for its various law enforcement and national security agencies. At the same time, however, the attorneys general in the various states have been responding to slow action at the federal level by taking on more responsibility for consumer enforcement in everything from policing Wall Street to suing drug makers for blocking lower-cost competitors. The distribution of power is constantly shifting, and sometimes, as at the moment, it moves in different directions simultaneously. In addition, the private sector today is often very much involved in carrying out government activities with government funding, so even the line between the government and the private sector is eroding.

For an ordinary citizen trying to get answers to a specific problem, this can be confusing and exasperating. This is why, when I was in Congress, my staff and I spent so much time directing constituents to the office and the level of government (or even private sector group) that could best help them. It can also lead to conflict within the system, as when states sue a federal agency they believe has failed to live up to its responsibilities. But rather than being a fundamental design flaw, the flexibility created by our Constitution allows for a pragmatic response to the evolving challenges we face as a nation. It creates the chance for policymakers to gauge whether problems are best confronted in town halls or state capitals or Washington—or in some combination of all of them—and then to work together to assign each level of government its appropriate role. That these roles change over time is a sign not of weakness but of the system's enduring strength.

Key Power:
Passing the Basic Laws of the Land

When a country is being organized, one of the most basic decisions is who makes the laws. The lawmaking body could be the king, the party secretary, the supreme council, or the militia, but in our system of government, it's the Congress. The very first thing our Constitution does is to grant Congress the core power of making the basic laws of the land, declaring in Article 1, Section 1 that "All legislative powers herein granted shall be vested in a Congress of the United States."

Certainly the president plays a very important role in the process, setting his agenda for the nation, recommending bills to Congress, threatening to veto legislation he opposes. But the main lawmaking responsibility rests with Congress, and its powers under the Constitution are awesome. Formally, it has the power to wipe out with a single law the entire executive branch, except for the president and vice president, and to abolish all federal courts, except for the Supreme Court, which it could reduce to a single judge with minor jurisdiction.[6] Many of Congress's legislative powers are specifically listed in the Constitution; others are implied. Over the years the courts have interpreted Congress's powers in such sweeping terms that it can legislate in almost every aspect of American life.

Lawmaking can be a complicated and intimidating process; one congressional report listed more than one hundred specific steps a bill might go through in the process of becoming a law.[7] But at its core—as I would often point out in my high school assembly speeches—it simply means trying to understand the hopes, needs, dreams, and desires of the American people and translating that into public policy through the legislative process. The American people tell members of Congress to do or not to do certain things, and they express basic interests and values. It is these experiences which are the basis of lawmaking.

But lawmaking is not done in a vacuum. It is carried out in an intensely partisan atmosphere, with one party competing against another, in very hard-fought battles. People feel deeply on both sides of the issue, and a lot is at stake—huge amounts of money, special programs, new benefits. In the legislative process, worthy groups compete for limited resources: younger people want more for education, for example, while older people want more for Social Security and Medicare. The place where we work out worthy, though conflicting, goals on the national level is Congress. The process produces winners and losers and can generate hard feelings, often lingering for some time, which is why a skillful legislator always tries to minimize the impact on the losing side.

The legislative process can be drawn out, untidy, and contentious, because Congress is trying to make the laws for a very large, highly diverse country. The complexity of the process reflects the complexity of the country. In a democratic society, the role of government is to moderate the tension among competing interests and to make it easier for people to strive toward the kind of life they want to lead. It is not easy, but it is essential that the tensions and the strife within a country of 300 million people be harmonized and accommodated. Congress's process of extensive deliberation, negotiation, and compromise often works, but not always. The great blot in our nation's history, the Civil War, showed all too painfully what can happen when social conflict cannot be resolved through the normal congressional process.

Ever since its first major bill—the Tariff Act of 1789, which imposed duties on imported goods in order to finance the new government's functions—Congress has approved more than 50,000 bills on every conceivable topic. In my very first Congress, I cast votes to pass the landmark Voting Rights Act of 1965, to set up Medicare and Medicaid, to approve the first general federal aid to elementary and secondary schools, to approve the student aid program for undergraduates, to set up two new cabinet-level departments (HUD and Transportation), and to pass and send to the states the Twenty-fifth Amendment to the Constitution on presidential succession, among many others. Legislators never cease to be amazed by the incredible variety of issues coming before them.

Giving this core lawmaking power to Congress was a major experiment by the framers, but it has generally served the nation well. As will be explored further in chapter 3, the process through which Congress reconciles competing views and makes the basic laws of the land is dynamic, complex, and untidy. Yet in the end I believe it is reasonably—not perfectly—responsive to the expressed desires of the American people. And it has generally—not always—allowed our nation to work through our differences peaceably for more than two hundred years. Above all, it is an ongoing process, for in a democratic society no issue is ever settled once and for all but is revisited again and again.

Key Power: Controlling the Purse

Ask the average American what Congress accomplishes, and the answer usually comes back: not much. Progress in Washington can be slow, with strong differences of opinion among legislators reflecting the fact that they deal with a large number of exceedingly difficult problems and come to the nation's capital representing all corners of our nation. Some issues on the agenda—like abortion—keep coming back for years, even decades, and never seem to be resolved. Yet on one of its most important responsibilities, Congress year after year is able to overcome differences and in the end reach an agreement that helps set national priorities.

That responsibility is Congress's "power of the purse"—its ability to set the spending and taxing policies of the nation. Not one dime can be spent from the federal treasury without the approval of Congress. The determination of the budget is usually the most important political process in Congress any given year, partly because of its size (more than $2 trillion) and partly because it is the principal means by which government establishes its priorities.

The framers of the Constitution, mindful of "taxation without representation" suffered by colonists under the British, took care to specify in the Constitution that the ultimate power to tax and spend resides in the hands of the legislative branch—which is closer to the people—not the executive branch. And it is without doubt one of Congress's most important powers. In the *Federalist,* James Madison called it "the most complete and effectual weapon with which any constitution can arm the immediate representatives of the people."[8] It checks the power of the president and gives Congress vast influence over American society, because federal spending reaches into the life of every citizen.

The annual consideration of the federal budget is an enormously complex undertaking—even more difficult to explain than the process through which a bill becomes law—and it can be highly contentious. The budget submitted to Congress by the president is often proclaimed "dead on arrival" by the opposition party; headlines throughout the year declare that the president and congressional leaders "clash on spending," and competing factions warn that if they don't get their way, a budgetary "train wreck" will occur and the government will shut down.

That rarely happens, and even if it does, the deadlock doesn't last for long. To be sure, the movement toward compromise may sometimes be slow and tortured. But in the end, the House and Senate reach an accommodation with each other, and with the president, that enables the federal government to meet its responsibilities from programs as large as Social Security and national defense to activities as small as repairing the panda cages at the National Zoo.

I don't want to overstate what Congress does. The vast majority of the spending items in the president's budget submission to Congress are approved every year. Congress will debate his budget and make various revisions, but most years the president largely gets what he wants. In many respects he is the chief budget maker, and Congress is the chief budget approver. The work involved in doing this is arduous, and—a reflection of its importance—it is the single most time-consuming thing Congress does. One veteran observer of Congress, asked to estimate how much time members spend on budgetary matters, replied: "Almost all." That's an exaggeration, but it may not seem like it during those many weeks each year when Congress is preoccupied with the budget resolution or the appropriations bills—sorting through thousands of recommendations, holding hundreds of hearings, casting hundreds of votes. In recent decades, about half of all House roll call votes have been budget related; in the Senate the percentage is even higher.

The multilayered congressional budget process has its shortcomings. And it is so complex and unwieldy that it is difficult for legislators, let alone the public, to follow. Constituents, who would often be confused by the work of Congress, would be overwhelmed by the complexities of the budget process, as well as by the amounts of money involved. Billions of dollars are so outside their experience that their eyes glaze over as politicians start talking about budget figures. As one constituent said to me in exasperation, "What difference does it make—a few million or a few billion?"

The average American may not know all about the several thousand pages of the federal budget, yet in the end Americans do know that Congress perseveres and ultimately fulfills the major responsibility assigned it in Article 1, Section 8 of the Constitution—"to pay the Debts and provide for the common Defence and general Welfare of the United States."

Key Power: Shaping Foreign Policy

Once, when Harry Truman was president, someone asked him who made U.S. foreign policy. His reply was simple: "I do."

No president today could make that claim. Indeed, not since John F. Kennedy was president has foreign policy been the preserve of even a few policy makers, let alone just one. As our country engages the world with renewed vigor and interest after the September 11 attacks, this is worth keeping in mind. Congress, too, is an important player in foreign affairs, a fact that might seem inconvenient in a time of crisis but that actually benefits the country in many ways. It is worth remembering that in terms of foreign policy powers specifically enumerated in the Constitution, Congress was granted more than the president.

Presidents have never been particularly keen about this splitting of foreign policy powers between the legislative and executive branches. Early on, President Jefferson stated, "The transaction of business with foreign nations is executive altogether." A Reagan administration official put this sentiment more graphically: "Involving Congress in foreign affairs is like having 535 ants sitting on a log floating down a turbulent river—each one thinking he is steering."[9]

There is no doubt that the president is the chief foreign policy maker. His control over the executive branch and command of the national stage give him enormous power to influence the foreign policy debate and to rally public and international support behind a particular cause. And in recent years Congress has devolved considerable power to the president to declare and wage war. Yet he regularly works within the framework of policies that exist in the laws passed by Congress. When Congress and the president understand their respective roles in foreign policy and make an effort to work together, better policy emerges.

True, it can be difficult for a president to work with Congress. For one thing, senators and representatives as a whole tend to focus more on domestic issues, just as their constituents do, and many give limited thought to foreign affairs except when a vote is pending or a crisis breaks. It is also true that power on Capitol Hill is diffuse, and it shifts with each issue. In the old days, the president could consult with Congress simply by talking to a few important congressional leaders and committee chairmen. Today, dozens of members of Congress and many congressional committees play major roles in foreign policy. Members are younger, more aggressive, better informed, more diverse, and less respectful of traditional authority. It no longer works for the president to consult with a handful of people and assume that the rest of Congress will go along.

We should also remember that the writers of our Constitution never envisioned an entirely unfettered presidency in foreign affairs. The president may be commander in chief, but the Constitution gave Congress the power to declare war, make the nation's laws, and pay for whatever policies the president pursues. The president has the power to negotiate treaties, but they cannot take effect unless the Senate ratifies them—and, in many cases, unless both the House and Senate pass laws to implement them. Without cooperation, in other words, some of the most basic tools of foreign policy cannot be used successfully.

And the plain truth is, no wise chief executive would want to try. American foreign policy always has more force and punch to it when the president and Congress speak with one voice. As the most representative branch of government, Congress best articulates the concerns of different segments of the population. When the president takes these views into consideration in formulating foreign policy, the policy that results is more likely to have strong public support.

During my years in Congress, I probably devoted more time to foreign affairs than any other single area. As a freshman member from rural southern Indiana, I wanted to serve on a House committee dealing with domestic matters, but for some reason never quite made clear to me, I was assigned to the House Foreign Affairs Committee. I stuck with it because I came to appreciate the important role Congress could play in shaping a sound foreign policy for the nation, both as an informed critic and as a constructive partner.

Yet throughout those years I was disappointed in every administration's consultation with Congress on major foreign policy issues. Often the administration contacted just a few select legislators, failed to consult on a regular, sustained basis, and frequently approached Congress after a decision had been made rather than seeking genuine input. Prominent examples of poor consultation were the Vietnam War of the sixties and seventies, and the Contra War in Nicaragua during the eighties. In both cases, policy was controlled by a small group of high-level officials, and few others either inside or outside the executive branch knew the full extent of our government's activities. It would be hard to argue that the country was well served by this approach.

Although it may seem awkward to have to consult with congressional leaders, presidents can profit from the experience. The president can be quite isolated in our system of government. As Lyndon Johnson's press secretary, George Reedy, once put it, in the White House no one tells the president to go soak his head. But members of Congress do not serve at the pleasure of the president, and that independence gives their advice added weight. The president may not like or take their advice, but he will probably forge better policy if he considers it.

On the tough foreign policy questions, the president needs help; the decisions should not be made by just one person. The framers wisely sought to encourage a creative tension between the president and Congress that would produce policies that both advance national interests and reflect the views of the American people.

Congress and Individual Liberties

Congress has clearly been given an extensive range of powers; some would say too many. One of my constituents would always comment how glad he was to see me back in Indiana, because then he knew Congress was not in session and was unable, as he put it, to "do any mischief."

A perennial constituent complaint is that Congress has too much power to interfere with personal freedoms. The perception is of a massively powerful institution that disrupts and invades our lives and undermines our individual liberties.

This is one of the most durable issues in American public life. Since the nation was founded, Americans have debated the proper balance between the rights of individuals to live their own lives and the power of Congress and the president to govern the country and make it secure. My guess is that we will continue to debate this question for as long as we endure.

That is because the founders themselves were unsettled on the matter. They wanted Congress to have extensive powers. But they were wary of granting it unfettered authority, particularly the ability to infringe too greatly on individual liberty. As Richard Henry Lee, one of the Virginia signers of the Declaration of Independence, wrote in 1787, as the nation was debating whether it needed an explicit Bill of Rights, "[T]he most express declarations and reservations are necessary to protect the just rights and liberty of Mankind from the silent powerful and ever active conspiracy of those who govern."[10]

Even the Bill of Rights, though, leaves a lot of room for interpretation. Ever since it was enacted we've gone back and forth on how far Congress and the president can go in abridging personal freedom, from the Alien and Sedition Acts over two hundred years ago, to our ongoing debates over gun control and abortion rights, to the more recent questions being raised over how far civil liberties can be trimmed in order to fight terrorism. The extent of Congress's power when it comes to individual rights is no cut-and-dried issue with easy answers. You could argue that debating it is fundamental to our character, a part of our genetic makeup as a nation.

This is true even though Congress's power is limited in ways that go well beyond the Bill of Rights. To begin with, the founders placed explicit restrictions within the body of the Constitution itself. Congress cannot pass *ex post facto* laws, for instance, or pass any bills of attainder—that is, legislation that declares someone guilty of an offense without trial. They also resorted to the core strategy of balancing power among Congress, the president, and the judiciary, making congressional action subject both to the president's veto and to the Supreme Court's rejection.

Congress is also hemmed in by political reality. It is a large body, with two separate institutions—the House and the Senate—each with its own traditions and temperament. They do not, by nature, see eye to eye, and each has its own crowded agenda of complex issues. Even within one chamber, finding common ground among all the various factions, regional interests, and ideologies can be quite difficult. People often complain about congressional inefficiency, but it is part of what safeguards our rights as citizens. Then too, forces outside Congress, from lobbyists and political parties to the overall judgment of the American people, constrain its actions. Simply put, once most Americans arrive at a firm opinion about a matter of public policy, particularly regarding their individual liberties, Congress will be hard-pressed to ignore it. Congress may be the most powerful legislative body in the world, but I can tell you from personal experience that anyone who serves in it also gets a keen sense of the limitations on its power.

This is a particularly tricky question when, as recently, there have been voices in the country at large pressing Congress to weigh in on the administration's efforts to prevent terrorist acts by broadening federal wiretap authority and expanding domestic spying capabilities. Others counter that Congress's role is simply to go along, but of course that's not so. It is one of the American system's marks of genius that we always have one branch keeping an eye on the other, and one of Congress's roles is to act on behalf of the American people as the guardian of our guardians: slowing things down when needed, requiring that fewer decisions be made in secret, guarding against unchecked powers. As Justice Louis Brandeis rightly observed, the American people "must look to representative assemblies for the protection of their liberties."[11] The founders may have wanted to ensure that Congress did not wield too much power, but they also did not want it to wield too little, which is why oversight of the executive branch is fully as important a congressional role as writing new tax law or appropriating money for new programs.

Whatever the challenge to individual liberties today from whatever source, members of Congress have to grapple with what's right for the country at the moment, just as we debated the Bill of Rights, just as we've argued over other civil liberties through the centuries. Woodrow Wilson once said, "The country is always aborning," and in this ongoing American experiment, the question of how far the federal government can go in impinging on individuals' lives is never resolved but must be taken up by each generation anew.

The Roots of Our Success

Almost any way you look at it, we have been a remarkably successful country. The twentieth century was clearly the American century. I don't want to join those who elevate the United States to near-holy status; we're certainly not perfect. At various times our nation's standing ebbs and flows, and we only do so-so when compared with other industrialized countries on basic social measures such as infant mortality or income inequality. But overall it seems fair to say that in the broad ways societies are measured—economically, militarily, the extent of our cultural influence, the freedoms we offer our residents, the opportunities we present for individual success—the United States has flourished over the past few decades.

Ask anyone why this is and you'll get a long list of explanations: the dynamism of our private sector; the sheer breadth and vast natural resources of this country; the creativity, vitality, and independence of the American people; the liberties enshrined in the Bill of Rights. Yet there's another important contributor to our success that I'll warrant would not come up often in conversation, at least not in this day and age: our government. In a recent survey, fewer than one in ten people saw Congress as very responsible for the successes the country has experienced in the past century.

This is not to suggest that people think Congress and the president are simply bystanders in securing the country's fortunes. It's just that after years of antigovernment rhetoric, deepening partisanship, widening special-interest influence, and saturation press coverage of political conflicts and personal scandals, our government and our system of representative democracy tend not to rank high on Americans' lists of why our country has been flourishing. This is too bad, because they belong near the top. The citizens of a country cannot have well-being without good governance. While market economies are important and the private sector is important, they cannot function without a framework, determined by government, and that framework is provided by representative democracy.

In essence, our form of government is our answer to the extraordinarily difficult question of how best to organize a society. Countries, city-states, and empires have wrestled with this issue over the course of history, and some have tried what amounted to disastrous experiments. Our system has succeeded in large measure because over the long term it has both promoted the dynamic forces within our society and provided a means of keeping them in balance. From its very beginning, our nation's government has been involved in defining the rights and liberties individuals could exercise, laying the groundwork for developing the country's resources, setting up the structure within which businesses could operate freely and fairly, and providing the security—military, judicial, and social—necessary for people to pursue their ambitions and take advantage of the opportunities afforded them.

We rely on our government, through our elected representatives, to sort out these difficult issues as well as to help us lengthen our vision for the future. As former senator Robert Wagner put it, "If a government or a people is to progress, its goal must ever be a little beyond its reach."[12] It did not have to be that way. Our country would be vastly different if the framers had placed power in the hands of a single ruler or given much less voice to the American people. As it is, though, the greatest secret to our success may not be that we get the balance among competing forces right all the time. Rather, it's that we have, in Congress, the presidency, and the judiciary, a forum for deliberation in which every American can have a voice in the process and a stake in the product. This ability to work together to resolve our differences and set the basic framework for the country is what helps our nation to flourish and allows us to live together so peacefully, productively, and successfully.

Even though Americans will often complain about government and not see it as much of a factor in our nation's success, it's where they turn when the big problems arise—war, disaster, terrorism, recession, disease—or when their local bridge decays or their retirement is threatened. The various ways the work of Congress has affected people's everyday lives is explored in the next chapter.

2

The Impact of Congress

WHEN I WAS IN CONGRESS, I would often start off my local public meetings by asking whether anyone could name a federal program that worked well. Usually not a single hand went up—even when the audience was filled with people who received Social Security checks every month, who drove to the meeting on the interstate highway, or who had attended the local university with the help of federal student loans. The response of my constituents was fairly typical. In a recent poll, when people were asked what they thought was Congress's most important accomplishment that year, more than three-fourths responded: "Don't know."

I recognize that it is commonplace to dismiss Congress as largely irrelevant or a bumbling institution that cannot do anything right. Yet people who have served in it typically come away with a different view. Claude Pepper, whose service in Congress representing the state of Florida spanned six decades, once remarked: "The government of the United States belongs to the people of this land and whenever their troubles and their disasters and their needs impel its use, it is available. It is the mightiest institution on the face of the Earth, and it can be a hand that will lift up the people if they call upon it."[1]

This chapter will explore this question of how much of an impact the work of Congress has on people's lives today.

Congress and the Fabric of Our Lives

Like many Americans, I watched the electrifying march of the U.S. women's soccer team to victory in the 1999 World Cup with a mixture of awe and pride. I was taken, of course, by the athleticism and skill shown by our players, but I was equally delighted by something most Americans probably didn't recognize: the role that Congress had played in what I was watching.

It has been more than thirty years since we passed the measure known as Title IX. I was still a relatively junior member of the House when we voted on the bill, and although the rhetoric on the floor was high-minded and full-blown, as it tends to be at such moments, I'm not sure anyone fully grasped the depth of the changes we were enacting. It takes nothing away from the extraordinary accomplishments of the women on the soccer field to say that they and those who celebrate their accomplishments could thank Congress, in part, for the path that led them there.

"Title IX" refers to a law passed in 1972, a set of education amendments to the Civil Rights Act of 1964. It requires that women be given an equal opportunity to participate in all programs run by colleges and schools that receive federal funds. One of its results, the full measure of which we are just beginning to enjoy, is the explosion of women's sports. In the wake of the U.S. soccer players' victory, President Clinton referred to them as "Daughters of Title IX," and he was right.

It has been popular of late to view Congress as full of people who love the limelight and look out for themselves but who contribute little to the national well-being. Not long before I left Congress, for example, a group of constituents visiting my Indiana office told me exactly that: Congress has nothing to do with our daily lives, they informed me, except when it wants to tax or regulate us. As it happened, I knew these people fairly well, so I responded by asking them a few questions—about the interstate highway they took to my office, the once-polluted river they crossed over, and the bank or grocery store or pharmacy they were going to next. They soon saw where I was headed. Their lives had been profoundly affected by Congress. If you know how to look, I suggested, you can see Congress's contributions all around you.

Just what those contributions ought to be, of course, is the subject of serious debate, and rightly so. Americans have this conversation all the time, in Washington and at political gatherings around the country, and it is how we remain on course as a nation.

But too often of late we've gone beyond that, to thinking of Congress as an irrelevant institution with little or no connection to our everyday lives. So as you hear about the work of Congress on all the issues facing it—tax cuts, national security, the federal budget, health care—think about how they might affect your life personally instead of dismissing the debates as esoteric and meaningless. What if Congress cuts federal funding for basic research into high technology and other sciences? Will it just be trimming unneeded fat from the budget, or will it be doing away with work that could undergird our growth in the twenty-first century—and possibly, a few years down the road, provide you or someone in your family with a job? Or think about health care: Should Congress continue to help researchers who are looking for a way to cure AIDS or breast cancer or any of the other diseases that cause us to suffer? Or education: Should Congress find ways of helping parents choose the best school for their children, even if it means using public funds to allow children to attend parochial schools? These are hardly questions that are irrelevant to our daily lives.

But this is what Congress does. When it takes up issues like the education of our children, or the quality of the water we drink, or our ability to care for our parents as they age—or whether women should be treated equally by college programs—it is doing its best to reflect and to improve the quality of our lives as individuals and the strength of our nation. So as the budget and other issues come up for debate in Washington, and those of us who pay attention to such things start discussing them with our friends and neighbors in community halls and meeting places, we should be careful about falling into the trap of believing that nothing is at stake.

Government's Greatest Endeavors

Skepticism toward government has always been a healthy strain in American thinking. The Constitution, with its emphasis on dividing government as a way of checking official power, is one reflection of that view. In recent decades, we have seen the relative optimism about government of the early 1960s give way to a broader pessimism, with many believing that government creates more problems than it solves.

Government is certainly not perfect. There are inefficiencies, mistakes, and blunders. We should not overlook these, but neither should they form the overwhelming impression of what government does. A recent study on government's greatest achievements over the past half century reminds us that there is another side to the story.[2]

The study developed a list of more than five hundred major laws passed by Congress in the past fifty years and then surveyed hundreds of college professors, asking them to rank the greatest achievements. The national problems and challenges that spawned these laws were as complex and difficult as the legislative solutions themselves. High on the list of accomplishments were rebuilding Europe after World War II through the Marshall Plan; containing communism and winning the cold war; maintaining the world's greatest defense system; expanding equal access and the right to vote; reducing the incidence of deadly or crippling diseases; increasing the stability of financial institutions and markets; improving air and water quality; protecting wilderness; providing financial security in retirement through Social Security and Medicare; expanding foreign markets for U.S. goods; promoting space exploration; and increasing arms control and disarmament.

As I look through this list, what strikes me is how our lives are better and safer in many ways because of government activity. Granted, an equally interesting study could be done on government's greatest failures over the past half century. Yet the report is still a helpful and all too infrequent reminder that as a nation we have come far in seeking to end difficult and deep-seated problems both here and abroad. And that's the key point. America rightly emphasizes individual values and independence, but when epidemic disease threatens our health, when dangers lurk at our borders, when energy shortages develop, when foreign trade barriers harm our exports, or when business irregularities undermine investor confidence, part of the way to cope with these problems more effectively is through action in Congress.

Certainly not every action by legislators is a blockbuster. Paul Douglas, the distinguished senator from Illinois, once commented that when he was elected to the Senate he came with the idea of saving the world. After a few years, he decided he would be content with saving the United States. After ten years in office he hoped he could save Illinois, and when he was leaving office he said he would settle for saving the Indiana Dunes.

The truth is, progress is usually made inch by inch. Issues often need to be revisited more than once, and setbacks are at least as common as triumphs. Yet as America faces a host of challenges in the twenty-first century, we need a broader public recognition that while government may be part of the problem, it is also part of the solution.

An Ordinary Day

From time to time, some major event comes along to remind us of how much we actually depend on the U.S. government. So it was that, after the Oklahoma City bombing and again after the

September 11 attacks, public support for Congress and the federal government rose to its highest levels in years.

I'm always encouraged to see this support, but to my mind it misses a crucial point. Congress and the president aren't just there on those days of crisis that are forever etched in our memory, nor do big-ticket items such as the military or homeland defense tell the whole story of government's impact on Americans' lives. Rather, working with the president, Congress has found many important ways to improve the quality of the average person's life. Imagine an ordinary day, and I think you'll be astounded at how much you can take for granted that your parents and grandparents could not.

Let's start the moment you wake up in the morning. The radio/alarm clock that just went off? If you live in a rural area—or in a suburb that twenty years ago was farmland—you might give a thought to the 1936 Rural Electrification Act, which brought electricity to rural areas and promoted the development you've been able to enjoy. If you live in a city, congressionally mandated subsidies and regulations have played no small part in bringing that power to your electric outlets at a price you can afford.

Now that you're up and brushing your teeth, it wouldn't hurt to remember the 1974 Safe Drinking Water Act, which put the government in the business of setting standards for drinking-water quality and making sure they're met. We take the safety of the water that comes out of our taps for granted, but before that law's passage, potential cancer-causing chemicals were showing up in cities' water, lead from supply pipes was becoming a problem, and viral and bacteriological contamination of water in smaller communities had been growing. While you're standing in front of the mirror, it's also worth remembering that a great deal of what we've learned about curing disease and remaining healthy has come from research funded by Congress. Moreover, if you wear cosmetics, take vitamins, or use medications, they have had to run a gauntlet of safety tests because at some point in the past, horror stories about their lack of safety led Congress to react. So, too, when you sit down at the breakfast table, you're benefiting from meat and egg inspections carried out by the Department of Agriculture and agricultural programs run by the federal extension service in every county.

Now let's say that, like most commuters in the country, you drive to work. Almost every safety feature of the car you drive, from the seat belts to the air bags to the quality of the tires, has been strengthened either by congressional mandate or by the activities of the National Transportation Safety Board. Your car's fuel efficiency has grown because of congressional pressure on auto manufacturers, as has the quality of the air you breathe. Many of the roads you drive on, of course, were funded by Congress. And if you're riding mass transit, federal subsidies played a big role in allowing the system to exist in the first place, and federal laws regulate its safety.

Once you get to work, it's hard to turn around without encountering some way in which the federal government has improved your lot in life. From improving workplace safety to prohibiting job discrimination, protecting your pension, or providing federal support for the industry you work in or the industries your job depends on, your working life has been shaped by congressional action. This is just as true of your education before you began working. Your high school likely enjoyed federal support for everything from its library to its lunch program; the land grant college system was established by Congress, while other colleges and universities depend heavily on federal research grants; and your college tuition may well have been supported by a Pell grant or some other federal subsidy, as today some three-fourths of all student financial aid in the country is financed by the federal government.

Finally, let's take a moment to think about all the things you do outside of work or home. If you enjoy parks, or like to boat on unpolluted rivers, or use community centers, or go online in the evening, or write checks from your local bank, or have some portion of your investments in stocks, or buy your children toys, or depend on food labeling to help you decide how to feed your family, you owe a moment's thanks to Congress for the funding or the regulations or the organizations that make it possible.

To be sure, there will always be room for argument about how the federal government goes about these various responsibilities. Certainly the government doesn't always get it right or do it in the most efficient manner. People can legitimately disagree about whether this federal agency has gone too far in regulating the workplace or that one has not gone far enough in protecting the environment. But the impulse that lies behind federal action—the desire to produce a higher quality of life for all Americans—is much harder to argue with. There are issues of reliability, safety, and comfort you don't even notice today, because at some point in the past, someone in Congress took note and did something about them.

Congress Does More Work than Meets the Eye

Make a joke about politicians bickering in Washington and a "do-nothing Congress," and audiences will always chuckle and nod in agreement. This criticism is as old as the republic, and it is one that resonates. Harry Truman's 1948 denunciation of the "do-nothing Congress" was the campaign slogan that fueled his come-from-behind victory over Thomas Dewey. Newspapers have been eager to reinforce the theme, with headlines like "The Do-Nothing Congress? It's a Good Thing" and "Here's to a Do-Nothing Congress." Lately it seems that Americans' historic skepticism toward Congress has evolved into something more sinister—sheer cynicism.

It is true that sometimes Congress doesn't have a stunning record of accomplishment. It usually has a long list of unfinished business. Members themselves are acutely aware of this. Many times throughout the year—during weekends at home or holiday recesses—they appear before constituents and are asked simply: "What have you people in Congress accomplished?" Even leadership-supplied lists of talking points may not give legislators much help in coming up with anything close to a convincing response.

So I think it's important to point out two things about Congress. First, it is capable of passing legislation with sweeping impact on the lives of Americans, particularly if there is a clear national consensus behind an idea or if action is imperative due to an external crisis. And second, even when Congress is not producing blockbuster bills, members are typically working on scores of other, less-publicized matters that sustain and improve the quality of life here and abroad.

It's remarkable how quickly we forget that Congress has been involved in some big things in the last few years—from overhauling the welfare system and rewriting telecommunications laws to liberalizing trade laws and expanding NATO. If the current Congress passes few landmark bills, is it fair to say that members have failed to earn their pay? No. Some of their work involves laying the groundwork for future action on very complex matters that may take more than one Congress to resolve. The Clean Air Act and Immigration Reform Act, for instance, took multiple Congresses to complete due to their inherent complexity.

At other times, Congress is grappling with issues on which the citizens of the United States as well as the political parties strongly disagree, and achieving compromise is difficult. For most recent Congresses, voters stacked the deck against decisive legislative action by choosing a Congress led by one party and a White House occupied by the other. Congress's critics say "politics" is to blame for the deadlock, but look at it another way: Parties in a divided government are laying out their arguments on issues to voters, asking them to deliver a verdict at the polls in November that could help resolve the impasse. That's democracy in action. This process may be slow and frustrating, but democracy is like that sometimes—actually, much of the time. It's a tough job trying to make public policy for our nation, especially in the absence of clear and decisive signals from the voters.

Reporters tend to make premature judgments midstream about "do-nothing" Congresses and then cover the high-profile issues that provoke legislative conflict. The inclination of the media is to show what's wrong rather than what's right. Far less attention is given to the routine but vital work that Congress does in other matters, most notably the annual appropriations process, which funds the wide range of federal functions that touch the lives of every American. Every session of Congress passes legislation to fund the departments, agencies, and programs of the federal government, based on scrutiny of past performance. Moreover, dozens of bills are enacted that are bipartisan and noncontroversial in nature, and even though many may be more modest in scope, they still address specific problems and needs. And each year, Congress holds hearings to air major differences of opinion, oversees executive branch conduct, reviews treaties and presidential nominations, and addresses constituent problems.

Some Congresses certainly may seem less productive than others. Yet it is still unusual for the legislative output in any Congress to fall much below four hundred new bills passed and signed into law, and rarely does Congress adjourn without enacting at least a handful of major new laws over its two-year cycle. Members, after all, recognize that they are legislators and their responsibility is to produce. Even when a Congress doesn't earn a big place in the history books, more is going on in the Congress than is often recognized.

A Balanced View of Congress

When I was in Congress, a curious thing would happen several times a year. A group of financial professionals would visit my office, sit down with me, and ask for some small change to the laws affecting them. What was strange about this was not that they were lobbying me—lots of people did that—but how they did so. Most groups, when they get a chance to meet a member of Congress, are curious about lots of things, especially the big issues: the economy, the deficit, foreign affairs. This group, though, only wanted to talk about the one seemingly minor change affecting their profession, with very technical legislation and very specific language in mind. Once that was done, they would go on to the next congressional office.

Now, they were doing nothing improper. But their lack of interest in the bigger picture struck me. When professional groups focus narrowly on their own interests, it's usually a sign that Congress needs to weigh their proposals carefully and look at the broader national interest. Sometimes, though, Congress fails to do this. When that happens, the results can be painful: Witness the recent corporate scandals coming after Congress's indulgent treatment of the financial and accounting communities.

This is worth remembering, because it hints at a reason why Congress can make mistakes. Critics of our national legislature often try to paint it as aloof from the cares of Americans, a distant and unapproachable institution. In fact, the opposite is true: Congress is highly responsive to pressure. Sometimes that pressure comes from all directions, as people in every walk of life weigh in on a matter they care about deeply; sometimes it comes from a single source that no one else much notices.

In many cases, this process has produced laws and innovations of which we can rightly be proud. But sometimes it results in Congress approving legislation that doesn't pass the test of time. Our founders made Congress a deliberative body in which legislation can take months and even years to pass in large part because they were aware of this and wanted to make it difficult for Congress to head off in a misguided direction. Even so, it happens.

In fact, it's not hard to come up with a long list of congressional actions—or cases of inaction—that with hindsight look quite unfortunate. Take this country's history of mistreating Native Americans through policies that were set by Congress. High protective tariffs in the 1930s, passed by Congress to protect various U.S. industries, deepened and lengthened the Great Depression. Prohibition passed in 1919, only to be repealed a decade and a half—and many violent episodes—later. Our failure after World War I to ratify the treaty setting up the League of Nations stemmed from Congress's decision not to engage the world through an international organization, a judgment that in retrospect may have helped usher in World War II. In the past ten years, Congress has frequently sidestepped difficult issues, doing little about the large number of Americans without health insurance, the long-term threats to the solvency of Social Security, and our dependence on foreign energy sources.

There are plenty of reasons Congress gets things wrong. Sometimes its workload is so heavy that issues don't get the thorough consideration they need. Sometimes the questions it takes up are so complex, and the competing interests are so diverse, that honest attempts at legislating a solution will fail. Sometimes there are political calculations or trade-offs that produce less-than-perfect results. And sometimes Congress is simply trying to develop policies that it thinks reflect the interests and desires of specific groups of people, yet do not serve the interests of all the people. It is a reminder that Congress—for whatever reason—makes mistakes, even with procedures and motivations that in other circumstances can produce solid results.

One of the most enduring features of the legislative process is that issues are revisited again and again. Even when Congress acts in the right way—such as passing Title IX to ensure that women are treated fairly in college programs and athletics—it still needs to go back later to make sure everything is working properly. Hence the appropriate review recently of whether Title IX has had any unintended consequences on men's athletics, exploring whether any adjustments or refinements might be needed. The same is true when Congress makes a mistake and gets something wrong. It needs to go back to the issue again and again, reassessing the options, trying to develop a sounder policy. All of this reinforces the point that the work of Congress is never settled once and for all but is always being revisited and refined.

Members of Congress Who Had an Impact

A few years back, *Roll Call*, which is a bit like the hometown newspaper for Capitol Hill, published a list of the ten most important members of Congress in the twentieth century. It included some familiar names—Lyndon Johnson, Hubert Humphrey, Robert Taft—and some names that people with a knowledge of American history would recognize, such as Joseph Cannon, the iron-fisted

House Speaker in the early years of the twentieth century, and Robert La Follette, the founder of the Progressive movement. As I read the article, though, I couldn't help but ponder how difficult creating the list must have been.

It's not fashionable these days to think of members of Congress as being influential. Sure, they might do something important for your community or have some authority within their committees on Capitol Hill. But many people would argue that, other than funding that handy new highway bypass or post office, the work of specific legislators has limited impact on the lives of Americans.

With all due respect, I disagree. Choosing ten names for the *Roll Call* article must have been difficult because it takes almost no effort at all to come up with a long list of members of Congress who have profoundly reshaped the lives of Americans, even going back into earlier periods of our country's history:

• In the very first session of Congress, for example, Virginia representative James Madison largely drafted and steered to passage the Bill of Rights, the first ten amendments to the Constitution which were ratified by the states in 1791.

• When he was speaker of the House from 1823 to 1825, Henry Clay of Kentucky developed his "American System" of national improvements, including a network of highways and waterways that greatly facilitated the movement of goods from farms and factories.

• In 1843, Representative Francis Smith of Maine led the effort to provide funds to Samuel Morse to develop a telegraph between Washington, D.C., and Baltimore, laying the groundwork for today's telecommunications industry. It was in an office in the Capitol that Morse a year later tapped out his famous message: "What hath God wrought!"

• During the mid-1800s, Congress was active in the expansion of the American territory. In 1859, Senator William Gwin of California first proposed to Russia the sale of Alaska to the United States.

• The nation's land-grant college and university system was created in 1862 through the work of Senator Justin Smith Morrill from Vermont, opening up higher education to the working class. That was 140 years ago, and yet there are hundreds of thousands of young people today who, were it not for Morrill's efforts, would have a much harder time getting a college degree.

- In one of the earliest efforts to protect America's stunning natural resources, Senator Samuel Clarke Pomeroy of Kansas led the effort in Congress in 1872 to set aside 2 million acres at Yellowstone as a public park for the benefit of the people.

- There isn't an American consumer who doesn't owe a debt to Senator John Sherman of Ohio, whose 1890 Sherman Antitrust Act opened up competition by eliminating business conspiracies that seek to monopolize the marketplace.

- Outraged by the looting of Indian cliff dwellings in the Southwest, Representative John Lacey of Iowa developed the 1906 Antiquities Act to protect battlefields, forts, canyons, and birthplaces of famous Americans as national monuments.

- In 1916, Representative Edward Keating of Colorado and Senator Robert L. Owen of Oklahoma were appalled by the widespread use of young children to work in manufacturing and industrial plants. Their Keating-Owen Act was the first federal effort to end child labor.

Other notable legislators since then include the following:

- Representative John Jacob Rogers of Massachusetts, whose efforts in 1924 led to the creation of the U.S. Foreign Service, giving the United States a well-trained network of diplomats all over the world;

- Representative Sam Rayburn of Texas and Senator George Norris of Nebraska, who brought about passage of the 1936 Rural Electrification Act, transforming the lives of millions of Americans;

- Representative Mary Norton from New Jersey, whose work as chair of the House Committee on Labor helped bring about passage of the 1938 Fair Labor Standards Act, setting the first national minimum wage;

- Senators Lister Hill from Alabama and Harold Burton of Ohio, whose 1946 act led to widespread construction of hospitals, particularly in rural areas, after World War II;

- Representatives Hale Boggs of Louisiana and George Fallon of Maryland, who shaped the 1956 Federal Interstate Highway Act, which has had an enormous impact on almost every facet of American life;

- Senators Hubert Humphrey of Minnesota and Everett Dirksen of Illinois, who were the pivotal sponsors of the 1964 Civil Rights Act, the landmark legislation that opened the door to racial equality in the United States;

- Representative Edith Green of Oregon, often called the "mother of higher education," whose Higher Education Act of 1965 created the federal student aid program, which has helped millions of undergraduates over the years.

The list could go on. But here's what makes selecting notable members of Congress even trickier. Working on specific pieces of legislation that change the country is important, but so is working to improve the institution of Congress itself. In the end, Congress is where the American people express themselves in all their diversity and come to some agreement on what to do about the problems of the day. If it doesn't work, then our republic doesn't work either. So to our brief survey I would add members of Congress who may not have a standout law bearing their name, but without whom we as a nation would be decidedly worse off:

- Richard Bolling, a brilliant Missourian who redesigned the federal budget process, making it far more thorough and accessible to the public, and whose knowledge of parliamentary procedure allowed him to push for congressional reforms over the years that made the institution itself far more responsive to the American people;

- Arthur Vandenberg, who exemplified bipartisanship by helping a president of the opposite party enact the Marshall Plan for European reconstruction;

• Carl Albert, a conciliator skilled at crafting compromises;

• Margaret Chase Smith, known for her courageous stand against the McCarthy hearings and their damaging impact on the institution of the Senate;

• Tip O'Neill, who defined the modern Speakership and knew how to make the system work;

• Mike Mansfield, Bill Gray, and Lindy Boggs—bridge builders who recognized the importance of developing consensus.

The American political system is built to move slowly so that Congress can guard against hasty action, take the time it needs to gain public acceptance for courageous legislation, and balance carefully the disparate forces in the country. Working within such a system is not easy. It takes enormous political skill to forge majorities, make the necessary trade-offs, assuage egos, and accommodate the different points of view. All of the legislators I've mentioned here—and many others like them—were able to manage that process. If Congress did not have people like them, the American political system would not work. I can't think of any greater measure of influence.

3

How Congress Works

W E HAVE ALL SEEN SURVEYS like those showing that 66 percent of Americans can name the hosts of various game shows but only 6 percent can name the Speaker of the House, and those finding that large numbers of high school seniors believe that big states have more U.S. senators than small states. Americans are busy people with many demands on their time, and it is not easy to put in a full day's work or finish hours of homework and then read an article about Congress or turn on C-SPAN to watch the House or Senate in session.

As a member of Congress I was never particularly disturbed by such survey results dealing with some of the basic facts about Congress. After all, more than one politician has been tripped up on the campaign trail by questions about some basic fact of everyday life, such as the price of a gallon of milk. What did bother me, though, was the extent to which people didn't understand or appreciate some of the basic concepts that underlie the workings of Congress. Even if you don't know the number of your state's senators or representatives, you should know something about what they do. Even if you don't know all the steps in the legislative process, you should understand something about the notions of developing consensus and reaching compromise in our system of government. If too many Americans get those sorts of concepts wrong, it *does* matter to the health of our system of representative democracy. This chapter will explore some of the basics about what a member of Congress does and how Congress really works—a view from the inside.

A Complex Institution

Seeing news clips of congressional bickering or stories about congressional gridlock, many Americans must wonder why anyone would want to work there. That puzzlement has been long-standing. "It's easy to see why a man goes to the poorhouse or the penitentiary," a nineteenth-century observer of Congress noted. "It's because he can't help it. But why he should voluntarily go live in Washington is beyond my comprehension."[1] Yet to those of us who have been privileged to serve in Congress, it is a fascinating and vital institution.

Since the very first Congress in 1789, some twelve thousand men and women have served in the House or Senate. Over the years, its members have ranged from framers of our Constitution and frontier explorers to astronauts and Internet entrepreneurs. From its ranks have come twenty-four of our forty-three presidents and twenty-eight Supreme Court justices. I was always struck by the varied backgrounds of my fellow members. It would not be un-usual to sit in a committee meeting with congressional colleagues who were once physicians, corporate CEOs, university professors, welfare recipients, social workers, professional athletes, physicists, or decorated war heroes. Former members of Congress invariably say one of the things they miss most is the daily interaction with their colleagues.

Congress is in many ways like a small city. More than thirty thousand people work in Congress, including auditors, legislative attorneys, caseworkers, library researchers, and Capitol police. Its buildings on Capitol Hill are spread over a forty-block, 250–acre complex, and most are connected by a labyrinth of corridors and underground tunnels. The Capitol building alone covers four acres. Its spaces range from the dramatic vistas of the West Front, where presidential inaugurations are held every four years, to the hidden, nearly inaccessible Intelligence Committee rooms, secure from even the most sophisticated electronic eavesdropping equipment.

Over more than two centuries, Congress has debated the structure of the new government, protective tariffs, Manifest Destiny, slavery and states' rights, declarations of war, civil rights and voting rights, articles of impeachment, and globalization. The main work of Congress is passing the nation's laws. In each two-year session, some five thousand bills will be introduced on the House side. And a comparable number of bills—often counterparts to House bills—will be introduced in the Senate. By the end of the two years, some five hundred new laws will be enacted, many of which will have multiple provisions incorporating several ideas originally introduced as individual bills.

Congress has two hundred committees and subcommittees to consider and prepare legislation, and members vote several hundred times each year on everything from routine procedural matters to resolutions of war or bills costing hundreds of billions of dollars. The variety of topics that come before Congress today is staggering, and moving bills requires a thorough understanding of a complicated legislative process with its own terminology—"mark-ups," "holds," "amendment trees," "filibusters," "cloture," "germaneness," "soft-earmarks," "suspension," "reconciliation," "PAYGO sequestration." When I entered the House, I was told in no uncertain terms to be quiet for my first few years until I understood Congress's rules and customs. Today's members become very active sooner, but there is still a fairly steep learning curve.

An Evolving Institution

Not fully appreciated is the extent to which Congress is an ever-changing, evolving institution. True, the core aspects of being a member of Congress have remained much the same since its first session more than two hundred years ago. If representatives or senators from an early Congress could be here today, they would still understand and appreciate the basics of congressional policy-making: the introduction of bills, the floor debate, the amending process, the House-Senate compromise, the possible presidential veto. They would understand the system's checks and balances and the important role Congress plays as the nation's premier forum for addressing the economic, social, and political issues of the day.

Yet many aspects of Congress have changed over the years, especially in the last several decades. During my years in the House I witnessed several major changes:

• *An expanded workload:* The workload of Congress has increased significantly over the years. Since I went to the House in 1965, the number of constituents that each House member represents has jumped by 40 percent, to an average of 650,000. The number of days in session, the number of recorded votes, the communications with lobbyists and constituents—all have increased sharply. Congress now receives 50 million e-mail messages and 200 million pieces of mail annually, compared with 10 million letters a year in the 1960s. The fax machines never stop running, and the phones never stop ringing. In my early years in Congress, I had one person handle all the correspondence; now most offices have five or six. And today Congress tackles a host of issues that didn't even exist in the 1960s—direct satellite broadcasting, ozone depletion, HMOs, cloning, AIDS research, computer privacy.

• *Budget process reform:* One of Congress's most important powers is its ability to set the spending and taxing policies of the nation. It seems hard to imagine now, but before 1970 Congress usually passed tax and spending measures without worrying much about their overall impact on the government's bottom line. The executive branch kept an accounting of whether the government ran a surplus or fell into a deficit at the end of each fiscal year. That changed in the 1970s, when Congress approved a series of budget-process reforms. Since then, lawmakers have made their decisions about spending in a much more coordinated and coherent way, with a close eye on how their decisions will affect, and be affected by, the economy.

• *A more complicated legislative process:* The movement of legislation through the congressional maze has never been more complicated, largely because Congress has made some major changes to the way it does business. In some cases, members have devised methods to circumvent the regular order, so they can move some bills through with minimal examination by their colleagues—including huge omnibus bills packaging together thousands of provisions and presented for just an up or down vote. In other cases, they have added procedural layers through their budget-process reforms, generating more points of order and additional motions and amendments. Filibusters, both formal and informal, have increased greatly in recent decades, which means the Senate now basically requires sixty votes to get anything done rather than a simple majority of 51. And the use of ad hoc committees to deal with special problems has greatly expanded, with the effect of further fragmenting responsibility for legislative issues.

• *Ethics reform:* Congress has tightened its ethics standards, an improvement that receives little public attention. When I came to the House, there were no financial disclosure requirements for members, no restrictions on accepting gifts or using campaign contributions for personal use, no written code of conduct, and no standing ethics committees to police the membership. All that has changed with a series of major reforms, primarily in the 1970s, which I was pleased to have played a role in helping to shape. Moreover, due to the well-trained eye of the media lens, members face more scrutiny than ever of their personal finances, campaign contributions, and office accounts. We have made important strides in reinforcing ethical behavior, though more certainly needs to be done.

• *Increased openness:* Congress has opened its proceedings in recent years, which is a bracing change. In 1965 no recorded votes were permitted on floor votes on amendments, so people had to be stationed in the House gallery to try to figure out how members were voting on controversial measures. That meant, for example, that we had to do a lot of thinking about how to get a recorded vote on the Vietnam War. At the time, the only way to oppose the war was to vote against the entire defense bill, which made it difficult for me because, although I had doubts about the war, I supported defense. It took a long time, but we finally passed procedural reforms that required roll-call votes on amendments. Today, House and Senate floor action is televised gavel to gavel, and votes are computerized so they are quickly and broadly accessible on the Internet. Some of Congress's key decisions are still being made behind closed doors, but almost all committee proceedings are open, and many are carried live on cable television or the Internet.

• *The decline in civility:* One of the more disturbing changes I've witnessed since 1965 has been the decline in civility among members. Certainly the history of Congress has been marked by rough periods, but too often in recent years politics has meant bitter partisan exchanges and mean personal attacks. We have sometimes seen more emphasis on questioning motives than on debating the pros and cons of the issue itself. One member coming off the House floor summed it up simply: "Man, it's rough out there." Spirited debate is appropriate, even healthy, and Congress remains a safe forum in which the conflicts within our society can be aired. But antagonism, incivility, and the tendency to demonize opponents all make it very difficult for members to come together to pass legislation for the good of the country.

• *A more representative Congress:* Congress reflects our country's diversity better today than in past decades, with far more blacks, women, Hispanics, and Asian Americans among its members, particularly in the House. Although further progress is needed, Congress is still one of the most representative institutions in the country. This change has directly affected congressional policymaking. In recent years, for example, there have been more than seventy women in Congress, compared with thirteen when I entered the House, and they have pushed to the forefront issues like gender discrimination, sexual harassment, breast cancer research, and family leave. Few politicians today would give a speech without saying something about the family, a major policy theme that only developed after women came into Congress. Almost certainly their numbers will continue to grow.

• *Electronic access:* During my early years in Congress, congressional offices used telephones, typewriters with carbon paper, and thermal faxes, which would transmit somewhat legible documents at a rate of three or four minutes per page (when they worked). Today's Congress takes advantage of the latest advances of the information age, and a new form of "electronic democracy" seems to be emerging. Individual members use websites, e-mail, satellite hookups, video conferencing, and chat rooms to communicate with constituents about what's going on in Congress. Some have set up live, interactive "virtual town meetings" via the Internet. On the various congressional websites, people can take a virtual tour of Congress, learn about the legislative process, obtain House and Senate documents, track the status of every bill moving through Congress, see live webcasts of hearings, and download hundreds of research reports on the major issues before Congress.

Over the next decades Congress will continue to change in ways we cannot predict or even imagine today. But it will still remain the protector of our freedom and the premier forum for addressing the key issues of the day.

The Many Roles of a Member of Congress

Ask most people what their member of Congress does on a typical day at work, and they're likely to say that he or she gives speeches, votes on issues, and sometimes shows up on TV or in the newspapers. Members do these things, to be sure, but that's just a fraction of what the job involves.

If someone were putting together a "Help Wanted" ad for the job of congressman, most members of Congress would say it would read something like this: "Wanted: Person with wide-ranging knowledge of scores of complex public policy issues. Must be willing to work long hours in Washington, then fly home to attend an unending string of community events. Applicant should expect that work and travel demands will strain family life, and that every facet of public and private life will be subject to intense scrutiny and criticism."

Being in Congress is hardly a lousy job. To the contrary, I found my work deeply fulfilling. But there were certainly times when I was frustrated by how little my constituents understood what I did and what the institution was all about. For all the media coverage of Congress, what members do on a daily basis still remains somewhat of a mystery to most people, even though several of those roles might be of particular benefit to them. Article 1 of the Constitution sets forth the powers of Congress and the qualifications necessary for election, but it contains no discussion of specific duties for the individual member. So in a sense members shape their own priorities. Yet they typically perform at least a dozen major roles:

• *National legislator:* Members spend a considerable amount of time on legislative duties, working to pass the laws of the nation and to determine federal spending levels for thousands of programs. During my years in Congress, the range of federal programs grew considerably, and a member's legislative responsibilities grew more complex and time-consuming. Our five hundred votes per year would cover a mind-boggling array of issues, from stem-cell research to education funding to human cloning to global warming. In the *Federalist,* James Madison wrote that a member of Congress needed to understand just three issues: commerce, taxation, and the militia. To a legislator today, that observation is a bit quaint, to say the least.

• *Local representative:* Each member represents his or her constituents in Congress. That means monitoring and seeking their opinions, recognizing their priorities, interests, and economic needs, and then trying to make sure that legislation passed by Congress reflects those perspectives. The founders were very clear that they wanted input from all regions of the country as Congress considered legislation.

• *Constituent advocate:* A member of Congress must be an advocate and ombudsman for individuals, groups, industries, and communities back home. This means everything from helping a senior who is having problems getting a Social Security check to helping a community obtain federal funding for a major new road. Because it's often difficult to figure out which local, state, or federal agency can help with a particular problem, people often start by asking their congressman. And as the federal government has expanded over the years, serving constituents and communities has become more far-reaching and time-consuming. In fact, members of Congress will sometimes complain that constituent service is crowding out the time they need to study legislation on which they must vote.

• *Committee member:* Committee work is one of the key duties in Washington. Each House member typically serves on two committees and each senator four, as well as several subcommittees. The point that Woodrow Wilson made many years ago—"Congress in session is Congress on public exhibition, whilst Congress in its committee-rooms is Congress at work"—is still largely true.[2] Although members must be generalists to be able to vote on the broad range of issues before Congress, they also tend to specialize in the areas handled by their committees, and develop considerable expertise in these areas.

• *Investigator:* Congress is charged with overseeing the operation of the federal government and in particular with ensuring that the president and the federal departments and agencies are carrying out efficiently and effectively the policies Congress has approved. This can mean everything from discovering that the Pentagon is spending six hundred dollars for a toilet seat to making sure U.S. intelligence operations are getting the right information to the right people at the right time. This work tends to be time-consuming and tedious, and pays few political dividends to individual members, but regular oversight of the implementation of laws stands at the very core of good government.

• *Educator:* Being in Congress also means being an educator, translating the work of Congress to constituents in an accessible, understandable way—sometimes through the media, most often directly. To be effective in this role, a member of Congress needs to establish a rapport with all types of people, from factory workers to white-collar professionals, from senior citizens to young students. I don't know of another job that puts you in closer touch with people—all kinds of people—than the job of a member of Congress.

• *Student:* At the same time, a member of Congress must also be a student of the views of his or her constituents. I quickly learned that no matter what the subject, there was always a constituent who knew more about it than I did.

• *Local dignitary:* A member of Congress must perform the ceremonial function of dignitary at home, serving as the "ambassador" from the nation's capital. The invitations never stop arriving, and literally 365 days a year could be filled attending community events back home. I often joked with constituents that I had been in more parades (thirty or more for thirty-four years) than any living American. If a member does not keep up a high profile at home, local wags say that he's come down with "Potomac fever" and forgotten the folks who elected him.

• *Fund-raiser:* As the cost of running for reelection has risen sharply—in my own case, it went from $30,000 in my first race to $1 million in my last—members have had to spend more and more time raising funds for their campaigns. To put this in perspective, running a $1 million campaign means that over the two years in a House term, you have to raise $10,000 from contributors every week.

• *Staff manager:* House members manage an average of seventeen personal staffers, while senators have forty. These aides work on Capitol Hill primarily on legislative matters, and in district or state offices mostly on casework and local projects. In addition, many members supervise committee staff, and those running for reelection also have separate campaign staffs. At one point, I had more than eighty staff people working for me.

• *Party leader:* Members are active in their party's caucus in Congress, attending meetings, helping to formulate a common position on pending issues, and working on strategies for the passage of particularly important legislative priorities. At home, members are involved in supporting local party tickets, broadening the party's base of support, and motivating voters.

• *Consensus builder:* The most effective members of Congress are skilled at bringing people together and finding mutually agreeable solutions to the various challenges facing our nation. It is extremely difficult in our diverse nation to forge consensus on complicated and controversial issues, and the tough work of hammering out compromise is almost impossible to accomplish in front of the TV lights. Those who are good at it often don't get public credit, since it's a job that is best done behind the scenes, in personal meetings with other members and their staff. Yet it is essential to the proper functioning of our system of government.

The demands on a member of Congress can be many and the personal moments few. But through these various roles, members receive an enormous amount of satisfaction in the part they have played in making the lives of people better and the country stronger.

Representing Constituents

Despite the complexity of Congress and its members' many roles, at its most basic the core responsibilities of members of Congress are two: passing and overseeing legislation, and representing their constituents. The framers of the Constitution viewed Congress as the country's policymaking engine and gave it broad legislative powers. Yet Congress is not only a legislative institution but also a representative one. Members are asked not just to pass laws but also to represent in Washington the interests of the districts and states they serve.

Thus one of the most perennially distressing poll results is the view that members don't care what ordinary citizens think. Polls consistently show that more than three-fifths of the public do not expect public officials to be responsive to their thoughts. In a 1996 survey, almost *half* of the respondents said they thought members of Congress would pay very little or no attention if they contacted them.

When I hear this, I often think of a conversation I had with Wilbur Mills, an enormously powerful legislator from Arkansas who had long chaired the House Ways and Means Committee. One evening we walked out of the Capitol together after a vote. His picture was on the cover of *TIME,* and he was known all over the country for his power over the tax code and his role in setting up Medicare. Powerful people sought his advice and clamored to speak with him even for a few seconds. I asked him where he was going and he said, "I'm going back to Arkansas. I'm holding a public meeting." He mentioned some small Arkansas town and said, "There'll be about fifteen or twenty people there." As we parted he said, "Lee, don't ever forget your constituents. Nothing, nothing comes before them." I never forgot it.

Having served with thousands of members over the years, my clear sense is that this attitude is the norm, not the exception. Members and their staffs put enormous effort into staying in touch with constituents back home, and they are probably more attuned to what their constituents think than at any time in the past. Most of them know their home turf very well. They know who its employers are, where its plants are located, and where people go for coffee in the morning; and they take frequent trips home to spend time in those places. A good friend of mine liked simply to head for the local shopping mall, where he would set up a table and listen to any comments people might have. Another made a habit of setting up a mobile office in the parking lot outside his state university's football stadium on game weekends. Members hold numerous public meetings, poll their districts regularly, and answer scores of letters and e-mail messages daily. They're on the telephone every day just to check up with constituents, and the door is always open to visitors from back home. Aware that the next election is never far off, members want to avoid being accused of "losing touch."

Besides, the vast majority of members are "of the community." Their roots—and often a large number of family members and close friends—are there, and they still maintain a residence in their home state. They know the area intimately because it is where they are from, and they have no desire to make decisions that will harm "their people" back home.

So why this impression that elected officials aren't representing the voices of common folk? Part of it, I suspect, is the general mistrust of politicians that marks this era in our history. Part of it, too, is that as districts grow larger and more diverse and as the issues besetting our country become more complex, it becomes harder for a member of Congress to know with assurance what constituents think about any single issue. But the biggest problem is that there is often little agreement among constituents on a given question. People often think that most of their fellow citizens agree with them about what is right and necessary, and they see no good reason why Congress shouldn't enact their point of view. Yet the fact is, it is very difficult to get agreement among a broad cross-section of Americans on any current major political issue.

Surveys over the years have shown that Americans don't even agree on what are the most important issues facing the country, let alone the best way to solve them. True, Congress was able to act forcefully in the 1960s to pass major civil rights legislation and more recently to respond to the September 11 attack, a reflection of the broad consensus that existed in the country. But in most years, when people are asked to identify the country's most important problem, they're all over the map. In a 1998 survey, for example, most of the respondents thought there was substantial agreement among Americans on the most important problem facing the nation. Yet when asked to identify it, no more than 10 percent of the respondents agreed on any single item.[3]

My own sense is that, if anything, members may be too responsive to constituents, paying attention to every shift in local opinion and every blip in the polls and thinking more about what's popular with their constituents than about what's good for the country as a whole. Abraham Lincoln once said that the art of democratic government is to be out in front of your constituents, but not too far out in front. Members are sometimes too close to their constituents, particularly when they risk reflecting their constituents' views at the expense of their own considered judgment—for example, going along with the popular conviction that Social Security should never be tinkered with, even when reform is clearly needed to prevent the program's long-term insolvency.

This is not a popular view. As one irate constituent shouted to his representative, "We didn't send you to Washington to make intelligent decisions. We sent you to represent us."[4]

But the founders didn't believe that Congress should simply mirror the will of the people. They believed it ought to "refine and enlarge the public view." They thought that members should favor the *national* interest in their deliberations. Yet it is not clear it has worked that way, as most members lean toward a local orientation, emphasizing their representative function. That's why people like their own representatives and senators, with well over 90 percent of those running again getting reelected. But it is also why national legislation aimed at the common good can get derailed for parochial interests, and why public opinion of Congress as an institution is fairly low. This basic tension between the representative and legislative functions of members has been going on for more than two hundred years, and it still remains today.

How a Bill Really Becomes Law

When I visit with students in American government classes, I always make a point of flipping through their textbooks to see the diagram illustrating "How a Bill Becomes a Law" in Washington. The diagram explains that a piece of legislation, once introduced, moves through subcommittee and committee, then to the House and Senate floors, then to a House-Senate conference, and finally to the president for his signature or veto.

Such diagrams can at times be helpful. But my basic reaction is: "How boring! How sterile!" The diagram can't possibly convey the challenges, the hard work, the obstacles to be overcome, the defeats suffered, the victories achieved, and the sheer excitement that attend the legislative process. It gives a woefully incomplete picture of how complicated and untidy that process can be, and barely hints at the difficulties facing any member of Congress who wants to shepherd an idea into law.

You don't just have an idea, draft it in bill form, and drop it in the House hopper or file it at the Senate desk. Developing the idea is very much a political process—listening to the needs and desires of people and then trying to translate that into a specific legislative proposal. Even the earliest stages of drafting a bill involve much maneuvering. The member needs to consult with colleagues, experts, and interest groups to refine and sharpen the idea; gauge the political impact and viability of the proposal (especially with constituents); determine how to formulate the idea so it appeals to a majority of colleagues; study how it differs from and improves upon related proposals introduced in the past; decide how broadly or narrowly to draft it (to avoid it being referred to too many committees); and decide how to draft it so it gets sent to a sympathetic rather than an unsympathetic committee. The Civil Rights Act of 1964, for example, succeeded because it was carefully drafted to avoid the Senate Judiciary Committee, where it would most likely have died; instead, its wording triggered a referral to the more agreeable Commerce Committee. To do this it avoided Fourteenth Amendment equal-protection arguments and instead relied on the federal government's power to regulate interstate commerce and in particular to prohibit discrimination in public accommodations—like motel and restaurant chains—that participated in interstate commerce.

Next, members don't simply introduce a good idea and then watch it move nicely through the legislative process. They need to rally support for the bill. The most time-consuming aspect of moving legislation is conversation: the scores—even hundreds—of one-on-one talks that an astute member will hold with colleagues to make the case for a particular bill, to learn what arguments opponents will use to try to block it, and to get a sense of what adjustments might be needed to move it along.

There was a time when it didn't take a hundred conversations to advance a proposal. If you could sell your idea to the leadership and one or two key committee chairmen, their clout would carry a bill well down the road to passage. Nowadays, though, more people on Capitol Hill have legislative power, including subcommittee chairmen, party leaders, leadership-appointed task forces, and individual members, especially those who are skilled at attracting media attention. You also need to consult people outside Congress, including key special interest groups who have much to gain or lose depending on the precise language of a bill and who have influence with members and extensive grassroots lobbying networks. Moving legislation today requires both an "inside" and an "outside" strategy—working to develop not only member interest but also public support. The media can be a powerful friend or a powerful adversary when trying to move legislation along.

Moreover, rather than expecting collegial acceptance of the idea, a member must be prepared to debate every line of a bill with his or her colleagues—certainly a formidable process but one that usually improves the final product. You need to develop the most persuasive arguments for the bill, be able to anticipate and respond to objections, consider which arguments or nonlegislative considerations might appeal to different colleagues, and find ways to demonstrate how the bill will help local districts.

The soundings from this smorgasbord of conversations generally wind up creating a dilemma: If you alter the proposal to accommodate skeptics you might broaden its appeal, but if you compromise too much you alienate core supporters. Successful legislators constantly count votes to ensure they have enough support, and they must be strategically savvy enough to determine whether they can mollify the opposition or must simply push ahead and hope to defeat it. They need to check with the parliamentarian to make sure that technical glitches do not undermine the bill. And they must consult regularly with congressional leaders, at a minimum to keep them advised if not actively involved. In the end it is the leadership that has the authority to make the vital decisions on when—or even if—to schedule a bill for floor debate and a chance at a vote on final passage.

All this adds up to a process that is extremely dynamic, messy, and unpredictable. There are ways for astute or powerful members to get around nearly every stage in the traditional model of the legislative process, making those "How a Bill Becomes a Law" charts of little value in predicting the path of legislation.

If with conversation, persuasion, persistence, and luck, a House member clears the many hurdles and gets a bill passed by that chamber, the reward is to begin the difficult journey anew in the Senate, where the threat of a filibuster immensely complicates the legislative process. Unless sixty of one hundred senators vote to close off debate on a measure, it is effectively blocked; the Senate on many issues no longer operates by simple majority rule.

The fate of a legislative proposal is also influenced by the preferences of the president and the executive branch bureaucracy. A member of Congress trying to advance a bill must take constant readings from the White House to learn if the president will veto it or sign it in its current form.

Guiding a bill from proposal to law requires energy, persistence, and competence. The legislative process is far from mechanical or automatic. Instead, it is dynamic, fluid, and unpredictable, with the outcome very much affected by the players—their goals, skills, ingenuity, and temperament. A skillful legislator must understand not only the basic mechanics of the process but also the personalities, the politics, and the strategies in order to succeed.

The workings of Washington sometimes appear to be a tangled and contentious maze, but there is a basic framework in which the action takes place. Granted, it is not as tidy as the textbook diagrams suggest; the legislative process is increasingly complex and dynamic and thoroughly political from beginning to end. But the structures through which a bill must pass have been set up to enhance the representative functions of Congress, with legislative efficiency taking a back seat. It is a process that goes to extraordinary lengths to take into account the need to hear from all points of view and to build consensus. Rarely is that quick or neat work, but it is the fundamental stuff of democracy, and it has served our country well.

Why We Need More Politicians

What this country really needs is more politicians! That was one thing I used to say to groups that was sure to get a reaction. When the snickers died down, I would explain that I was actually quite serious, that we do need more people who know how to practice the art of politics.

This is not a skill that has come in for much praise in recent years, but that's because we're confused about what it entails. When the federal government almost shut down a few years back, that was considered "politics." When Washington grew obsessed with the impeachment of President Clinton and the rest of the people's business took a back seat, that was "politics." Showing skill as "a politician" has come to mean demonstrating the ability to raise campaign funds, or to engage in the tit-for-tat exchange of negative advertising, or to jockey for public support based on polls and focus groups, or to skewer an opponent with a one-liner during a televised debate.

So we've come to view the word "politician" with considerable disdain. Yet none of this defines a good politician. Good politicians are vital to the functioning of our democracy, and we desperately need more of them. Let me give you an example of what I mean.

Suppose you're in Congress, and you decide to start focusing on our country's drug problem. Let's say, as well, that you firmly believe the answer lies in using federal funds to back more treatment programs for addicts. But then an interesting thing happens. As you talk to your colleagues, you discover that they're all over the map on the issue: Some support hard jail time for users; some want to beef up antidrug education efforts; some want to help law officers or to strengthen border patrols; others want funding for medical research into the causes of addiction; and still others want to focus on eradicating crops in Asia and South America. Gradually, it begins to dawn on you that to make progress on the issue, you're going to have to find a way to give others some of what they want as well. It's at this moment, as you set about crafting a bill that can take all these voices into account, that you'll begin to discover why true politics is considered an art.

There are plenty of people who would look at the process of reconciling these competing points of view as messy and unseemly. "Stick to your guns!" they would urge. "Anything less is a sell-out." But controversy and conflict in a large nation are unavoidable. To avoid ripping apart at the seams, our country needs people who know how to accommodate different points of view and work for common solutions. That is what good politicians do: They make democratic government possible in a nation alive with competing factions. Simply put, they make the country work.

Hardly anyone appreciates this. As we scrutinize members of Congress, we all but ignore their political skills. In the many years I represented southern Indiana in Congress, I participated in thousands of public forums, newspaper and television interviews, and radio call-in shows. But I can count on one hand the number of times I was asked questions that dealt with my political skills. People knew where I stood on expanding trade and helping seniors; they even knew I shared the Hoosier passion for basketball. But for the most part, they never asked me how good I would be at turning their concerns or mine into law or at advancing local and state interests among my 534 colleagues in Congress. For some reason most people and journalists seem to take basic political competence for granted.

They shouldn't. As hard as it is to get to Congress, doing a good job once you're there is even harder. The key is respecting the system and figuring out how to make it work. Frequently you will find people in Congress with high ideals, good ideas, and considerable energy, who nonetheless lose because they never figured out how to work the system to get things done. It takes being a good politician, in the best sense of the word: that in the face of the diverse beliefs and opinions represented in Washington, you can work with your colleagues to build support for an idea and move it forward.

So what should we be looking for in a politician, someone who is able to practice the art of politics in Congress?

First, they should know how to consult, particularly with their fellow members—talking to them, listening to them, making sure they feel they are in the loop. You build support for ideas one-on-one with colleagues and key individuals. They all have their own ideas and their own valid concerns; they expect to be able to share them, not simply to be lectured to. Lyndon Johnson had his own way of putting this, with the sign he had in his Senate office: "You ain't learning nothing when you're talking." Good politicians need to be able to hear from all sides, and they soon realize that you can never consult sufficiently.

Second, they should be able to calm rather than inflame the discussion of controversial issues. In public meetings in Indiana and in discussions in Congress, I often encountered people who were angry or felt passionately about a particular issue and might end up shedding more heat than light on an issue. I didn't always agree with my colleagues, but I tried to make sure the disagreements were honestly stated, orderly, and civil. I remember Carl Albert telling us to always respect our colleagues and never forget that each of them serves in this House because they were elected to do so by the American people.

Third, they should know how to persuade. It takes an enormous amount of work to build a majority's support for an idea. I once set out to push a modest piece of legislation having to do with reviewing the operations of Congress. It wasn't especially complicated, but by the time I was done trying to line up support, I'd been in touch with more than a hundred individuals from both parties.

Fourth, they should be willing to share the credit. I remember former Speaker Tip O'Neill putting his arm around me as we walked down the hall and giving me some advice. He called me Neal for my first decade in Congress because I reminded him of a Boston baseball player by the name of Neal Hamilton. "Neal," he said, "you can accomplish anything in this town if you're willing to let someone else take the credit."

Finally, they should know how to compromise. The public and the press try to lock members of Congress into more and more specific positions on the issues, well in advance of a vote. But good politicians search for the common ground among diverse views and know how to make adjustments to their proposals without betraying their core beliefs. One of the most misunderstood concepts in our system of government is the notion of compromise and reaching consensus, with polls showing most Americans think compromise just means selling out on your principles.

But compromise is essential to producing law in our system of representative democracy. Disagreements over views deeply held are unavoidable in a nation as large and diverse as the United States, and people will inevitably differ over means and ends. Good politicians are able to find the points of agreement that will allow a consensus to emerge, looking for solutions that allow both sides to claim, if not victory, at least some gains. It might be altering some key words, phasing in a change, inserting a new provision, requiring a study, splitting differences in funding, delaying or postponing implementation of a section. There is almost always a way to solve problems without confrontation, and part of the skill of a member of Congress is finding ways to resolve differences. Skillful legislators seek accommodations among rival interests, because they know that it's necessary to make the country work. Other issues will surely come along, and good politicians recognize that creating permanent enemies will make it difficult, if not impossible, to enlist their help in the future.

Of all the skills demanded of an effective member of Congress, developing consensus—bringing people together, accommodating different points of view, and finding acceptable solutions to our nation's problems—is perhaps the most important of all. It is why we need more politicians these days, not fewer.

Power in Congress

Central to being an effective member and moving legislation through Congress is understanding who has the real power in the institution. Sometimes it takes time to master an institutional nuance about power; sometimes you get the point rather quickly.

I remember getting a vivid introduction to how power works on Capitol Hill as a freshman member of Congress. Following the lead of the president, a small group of us introduced a measure to extend the term of House members from two years to four. Given its support in the White House, we thought we had a chance for success, so we were optimistic when we approached the chairman of the House Judiciary Committee, an awesome and fearsome New Yorker named Emanuel Celler. I was designated the spokesman for the group. How, I wanted to know, did Mr. Celler stand on the bill?

"I don't stand on it," he responded. "I'm sitting on it. It rests four-square under my fanny and will never see the light of day." He was right. It didn't. And we learned that day something about congressional power—that some individuals have enormous power within the institution either to move legislation forward or to kill it.

Whenever national attention focuses on Congress, it's crucial to remember that power is not equally shared within its walls. To understand why some proposals make it and some don't, you also have to understand who has the real power in Congress.

This is not quite as easy as it might seem. One of the most noteworthy features of congressional power is that it regularly shifts over time. In the nineteenth century, the Speaker of the House had enormous power over the membership, as you can gather from the nicknames of Speakers like "Czar" or "Boss." In the early twentieth century, a revolt by rank-and-file members shifted power to the committee chairmen, and in turn more power was given to individual members by the post-Watergate reforms of 1974. In the 1980s and 1990s, there was a sense that the decentralization of power had gone too far, and over the past decade the Speaker and his leadership team have once again become more powerful.

The truth is, though, that power in Congress shifts not only from one era to the next but also from one election to the next, as party strength and committee alignments change, and even from one issue to the next. One proposal might move through Congress because it's the priority of a powerful committee chair or is strongly supported by the administration. Another might move because its champion has a high media profile and the ability to command national support, even though he or she does not serve on the relevant committee. Yet another might pass because a determined voting bloc within Congress insists on its inclusion in exchange for their votes on the overall bill.

What makes Congress different from most institutions is that no one is in charge of the entire body. There is no CEO or person whose desk has a plaque reading, "The Buck Stops Here." There are easily identifiable leadership positions, of course, where the organizational charts tell you that power should reside. Yet despite their stature, their visibility in the media, and their ability to organize the chamber and schedule floor business, congressional leaders don't actually have much power to force members to act in a certain way. This is because Congress is highly decentralized, few members consider themselves followers, and the leaders do not have many formal powers to call upon. When he was Senate Majority Leader, Bob Dole would often say that a "p" was missing from his title—that he should have been called the Majority Pleader instead. When he was House Speaker, Carl Albert used to say, "I have no power but the power to persuade."

A basic truth in mathematics is that the whole is equal to the sum of the parts. Yet that has never applied to Congress. Members of Congress are a talented group overall, yet the institution itself doesn't seem to measure up to the sum of their individual talents. I'm not quite sure why that is, but part of the explanation might lie in the manner in which Congress is organized and power distributed.

The power of individual members comes from multiple sources. In the first instance, it derives from the fact of their election, which bestows a certain power both inside and outside the institution.

Obviously, it helps to hold a committee chairmanship or serve on particular committees, such as the "money" committees that in recent decades have become dominant on Capitol Hill—the Appropriations Committees, the House and Senate Budget Committees, and the Senate Finance and House Ways and Means Committees. But beyond that, particular members may be powerful because they are persuasive debaters or securely in command of the facts they need to convince others. They may be well liked or highly respected for their judgment or expertise. They may be media-savvy or close to the president or adept fund-raisers who can help out other members in their campaigns for reelection. In more recent days, the ability to raise campaign money has become the path to leadership and power in Congress. Power also rests in the hands of those who have effective political skills—the ability to listen, build coalitions, accommodate different points of view, and make compromises. And sometimes power grows out of members' experiences outside Congress—as Senator John McCain's years as a POW have given him enormous standing on defense issues—or because they speak for a major special interest group—as Claude Pepper once did for seniors.

Whatever its source, power is what moves ideas and legislative proposals along in Congress, and it is also what can slow them down. The key sources of power for every bill are different, as the mix of players involved constantly shifts, depending on the issue under consideration and the stage of the legislative process reached. All of this makes the legislative process very fluid, very dynamic, and endlessly fascinating.

The House and the Senate

People are surprised to hear that I authored one of the biggest, most comprehensive tax cut bills considered by Congress in the 1980s. Well, maybe not in the way you might expect.

Actually what happened was that I introduced a very minor bill, HR 5829, to provide some tax relief to the church I attended in

Washington, so they wouldn't have to pay high import duties on a new set of bells they had just imported from Europe. Under the division of responsibilities between the House and the Senate as laid out in the Constitution, only the House has the power to originate tax legislation. Since the Senate wanted very much to draft a major tax cut bill, particularly during the 1980 campaign year, they took my bill once it passed the House, basically deleted everything after the bill number, and in its place put their extensive tax cut language as an "amendment." So it was my modest HR 5829 which became the major vehicle in the Congress that year for debating tax cuts. My office obviously received more than a few puzzled calls about this. But the point is that the standard textbook lists of differences in roles and responsibilities between the House and Senate have become increasingly blurred in recent years.

Of all the changes in Congress since it was established more than two hundred years ago, the framers would probably be most surprised by how much the Senate has changed. The framers had divided up various powers and responsibilities between the House and the Senate, with the House, for example, originating revenue bills and the Senate approving treaties and presidential nominations. But they also viewed the two bodies as having two distinct roles in the basic legislative process: The House, whose members were elected every two years, was to be the closely connected to the needs, desires, and wishes of the American people and was to be the voice of popular opinion. The Senate, on the other hand, with its membership appointed by the states and with its six-year terms for senators, was to be the much more detached body that would take the legislation passed by the House reflecting popular passions and consider it in a more deliberative way.

The framers were very clear on the distinctive nature of the Senate. As George Washington explained, just as we pour coffee into a saucer to try to cool it down, "we pour legislation into the senatorial saucer to cool it."[5] Over the years, various changes to the Senate have eroded this key role, including ratification of the Seventeenth Amendment in 1913 providing that senators too would be elected by the people, thus making them much more responsive to popular opinion. It is still probably true, however, that House members tend to view themselves more as local officials—working on local projects, staying in close contact with county officials and mayors, emphasizing direct personal contact with the voters through scores of local town meetings—while senators tend to view themselves more as national figures. And House members are still generally more responsive to the latest blip in public opinion, while the Senate remains the more deliberative body.

Other differences between the two bodies range from the larger percentage of votes needed in the Senate to cut off debate and move a bill forward, to the tendency of senators to be generalists covering a broad range of legislative interests while House members tend to develop considerable expertise in the more focused areas covered by their committees. One of the more important differences relates to size. Because the House has many more members, House rules are stricter and give the majority party far greater power to move legislation. Floor consideration of legislation is generally highly structured in the House. The majority controls the procedures, and he who controls the procedure controls the results. If the majority party can hold its members together, the minority in the House is basically out of the game. On the other hand, individual senators—of both parties—have extensive powers in the legislative process, being able to debate any measure at length and to offer any amendments—even unrelated amendments—to whatever bill is under consideration. In general, House rules favor the majority—so the will of the people prevails without being blocked by the minority—while Senate rules give advantages to the minority so they can stop the majority from acting too quickly.

One constant is that each body continues to perceive the other as an obstacle to be overcome in the legislative process, with members often frustrated by the other chamber's procedures. Grumbling about the other body's handling of an important matter is commonplace. It's become almost a standing joke among members that it is the *other* body that is messing things up and is responsible for the ills of the legislative process. There is also a genuine competition between the two bodies—trying to be first to get the prominent witnesses, to move important legislation, to respond to national crises—which is by and large a healthy competition.

Most Americans take it for granted, but our truly bicameral system, with two chambers of equal power, sets Congress apart from almost any other parliament in the world today. The roles of the House and Senate may not be exactly the same as envisioned by the framers, but important differences remain, generally enhancing the overall workings of the Congress.

The Awesome Responsibility of Voting

As I was chatting with a constituent one day, he brought me up short with a simple question: "What's the toughest part of your job?" At the time, I'd represented southern Indiana in Congress for well over two decades, but I had to pause to sort through the possible answers. The long hours? The time spent away from home? The criticism? The heavy lobbying? Suddenly, it came to me that the answer had nothing to do with the frustrations of the job but with its essence: The toughest part of serving in Congress is voting on legislation.

Voting is an awesome responsibility, and it lies at the very heart of a member's duties. I remember my first vote as a new member in January 1965. It was to elect the Speaker of the House, which is an automatic, party-line vote for control of the House. But to this day I remember listening carefully as the name of each representative was called by the clerk and, eventually, I had to rise in the historic House chamber and call out the name of my party's candidate. One of my last votes as a member was on impeachment of the president, and I remember it too; it was hardly an auspicious way to end a voting career.

But voting is also a particularly difficult responsibility. This generally comes as a surprise to people. In the popular imagination, members of Congress don't have to work very hard to make voting decisions. They listen to their biggest campaign donors, or to powerful special interests, or to the polls, and then vote accordingly. Or perhaps they're captives of a particular ideology: Whatever the conservative or liberal line might be on a given bill, that's where they come down. As with many common perceptions about Congress, there's a germ of truth in all of this, but the reality is far more interesting.

Members recognize they are casting their votes to draft the basic laws of the nation, and they take this responsibility seriously. On average they participate in 95 percent of all votes held. They typically put a lot of effort into making sure they cast their votes in the most thoughtful and defensible way possible. They are well aware that they will frequently be called on in many different forums to defend how they voted.

Each vote has a different dynamic, and the approach members take in deciding how to cast it may vary, but in general the process includes several considerations:

First, as I've already suggested, members pay close attention to what they hear from their constituents and try to reflect the views of those who sent them to Washington. They get constituent letters, e-mails, faxes, and telephone calls by the hundreds or even thousands on some bills. Members also solicit constituent views through public meetings and questionnaires and stay on top of opinions back home by closely following local newspapers, media, and public opinion surveys. All too often, however, these constituent voices conflict with one another or are expressed in only the most general terms, so a member has to work hard to discern a majority sentiment.

Second, members get recommendations from a wide range of expert and political sources. They have stacks of background material sent by special-interest groups and think tanks; they can read page after page of testimony collected by congressional committees; colleagues in Congress send out letters with recommendations; the administration—and, on significant occasions, the president himself—will often weigh in as well. Members are aware of how their party's congressional leaders—as well as contributors to their campaigns—want them to vote on a particular issue. They also rely heavily on what like-minded colleagues or members with particular expertise think about an issue. It is quite common for members trying to make up their minds to seek the opinions of colleagues who are well respected for their issue expertise and have worked extensively in a particular area.

Third, members look beyond the recommendations to assess the major arguments being offered for or against a bill. The decisions can be difficult, since good points are often made on both sides of an issue. Members must sort through a host of arguments—legal, statistical, economic, moral, and pragmatic—and make a judgment as to which are most persuasive. After the vote is over and members have to explain their votes to constituents or to the media, they will almost always cite two or three of the main arguments or reasons they found most compelling.

Fourth, members bring their own core convictions and personal histories to the process. They don't come to Congress as blank slates, awaiting the directives of others. Instead, they may have strongly held core beliefs—such as the sanctity of life, the need for limited government, the imperative to help the less fortunate, or the importance of assisting a particular country or region of the world—that color their decisions on specific bills.

Deciding how to vote is complicated because it involves complicated issues. It is not as easy as the TV "sound bites" make it out to be. On some issues, members of Congress vote their consciences; on others, they follow what they think are the wishes of most of their constituents; on still others, particularly those votes that mean less to their own districts, they stick with their party leaders or some congressional faction, often in hopes of getting support later on a bill that matters more to them. Often, especially when the votes are coming quickly, they will take cues from respected like-minded colleagues. Sometimes, when a bill isn't of much consequence to particular members, they will respond to a colleague's plea on the floor: "I really need you on this one." Each bill that comes up involves a different calculation, but it always involves a calculation.

Imagine yourself in Congress, for instance, considering the Justice Department package of some forty changes to make it easier for law-enforcement officials to fight terrorism. Every day, your office staff has to deal with letters and calls from constituents urging you either to go along in the name of security or to proceed cautiously in the interest of safeguarding basic American liberties. Every day, you hear from a host of experts and interests from all sides of the issue advising you on the right course to take. An easy decision? Hardly. In the end, your vote will be black or white—you can only vote Yea or Nay—but casting it will have required a thorny analysis of shades of gray.

And this is just one issue. As a member of Congress, you cast hundreds of votes a year on everything from basic constitutional questions to cotton subsidies to tiny changes in a time zone. Moreover, sometimes you are faced with complex bills with hundreds of provisions, some of them good, some of them bad. Yet you must make a judgment on balance and cast one vote up or down. Though you may become well versed in many subjects taken up on the floor, you can't possibly get to know them all. And with all that is going on in Congress, finding the time to actually arrive at a decision can be a challenge. Yet on every single vote, you'll be expected to have an opinion and be able to defend it.

Members are intensely aware of the anguish their votes sometimes cause. A few years after I came to Congress, I offered one of the early amendments to reduce funding for our involvement in Vietnam, a move that put me squarely in opposition to the White House. We lost the vote, though we received more support than we had expected. I happened to go to the White House later that night. I'd been one of President Johnson's favorites from the House class of '64, and he had come to Indiana to campaign for me in 1966. He had taken a special interest in my career. I will never forget his eyes when he asked me, "How could you do that to me, Lee?"

The issues facing lawmakers when the time comes to vote are often complicated and numerous, and the recommendations and considerations can be varied. But in the end the final step is always the same. The member must make a decision and cast the vote, knowing that in our system of representative democracy he or she alone will be held accountable for that Yea or Nay.

The Frustrations and Rewards of Congress

I recently came across a letter from a well-known American politician to his wife. He was not impressed by the perks of his job. "The business of the Congress is tedious beyond expression," he complained. "Every man in it is a great man, an orator, a critic, a statesman; and therefore, every man, upon every question, must show his oratory, his criticism, and his political abilities."[6] Turn on C-SPAN any day that Congress is in session, and you'll see what that fellow meant.

What's interesting about this letter, though, is that its writer was John Adams, and he posted it to Abigail from Philadelphia in 1774, while the Continental Congress was in session. It's hard not to be taken aback by his dismay. This was, after all, an extraordinary collection of people bent on the extraordinary business of framing the charter of the new nation. Simply to be a part of it would have been exhilarating, you would think.

But then, some things have not changed in the 230 years since John Adams wrote that letter. In the popular mind, of course, being a member of Congress seems a glamorous and pampered job. There are the visits to the White House, the travel on Air Force planes, the big speeches, the media requests for statements on all sorts of issues, the sense of being at the center of big events and an initiate into the rituals of democracy. Being a member of Congress makes others pay attention.

Yet as a former congressman, what I remember just as strongly are the job's frustrations. Progress in a legislative body comes very slowly. You do things inch by inch, not mile by mile. A defeat on something you strongly believe in can be devastating. The hours are terribly long—made even longer by the fact that, when Congress is in session, you can never get away from the bells that tell you a vote is in progress and you have to drop whatever you're doing and run to the floor. This would be fine if the votes involved vital matters of state, but in a typical week you're asked to cast scores of inconsequential votes: procedural votes; votes that were brought up simply to please a tiny constituency; votes that are symbolic, not substantive; votes that the other party just wants to use to score political points.

Committee meetings go on without end, and the work itself is often tedious, requiring that you go over legislation comma by comma. You are constantly rushing from one meeting or appointment to another, and your daily schedule, meticulously worked out, is always being interrupted, revised, or simply scrapped. Constituent demands are unrelenting. If you have children, you're going to miss a good part of their lives, and with the constant travel, airports become as familiar as your home. You cannot plan ahead, whether for an evening off or for vacation, because some event or delay always demands that Congress stay in session longer than planned.

My wife can give you a long list of important family events I missed while I was in Congress, from church confirmations to honor society inductions (although I did make the graduations and the marriages). The first question I always ask someone telling me they want to run for Congress is: "How does your spouse feel about it?" Congress is tough on families. I came to Congress in 1965 with a very large freshman class; only a few of those marriages survived.

After a while, all the political posturing, sniping, and scrambles to claim credit for good things—or avoid blame for bad—become increasingly distressing, and the constant maneuvering for partisan advantage becomes ever more disheartening. And for putting up with all this, many members of Congress get paid less than they could make in the private sector and face harsh and frequent criticism.

Yet despite it all, most members run for reelection, many remain in office for decades, and there is always an enormous pool of talented people who want to serve in Congress. Why? Some like the trappings of power and the way the job feeds the ego; but most,

I think, are truly motivated by the belief that, hard as it is, they can make a difference in the lives of ordinary Americans.

Far from driving people out of politics, the give-and-take of public life is usually what most satisfies them. There is a pervasive sense on Capitol Hill that it is where the issues of greatest importance to the nation are being sorted out. Sometimes this is misplaced, but often it is not, because one of the things you quickly learn in office is that after two hundred years, we are still struggling over the questions that aroused the passions of this country's founding generation. How much power should the federal government be given? How far should government go in regulating our affairs or trying to better our lives? How do we resolve the tension between encouraging individual liberty and initiative and buttressing a central government strong enough to promote justice for all? John Adams, Thomas Jefferson, Alexander Hamilton, and James Madison tangled over these same questions. Our system's strength rests in part on the fact that these matters are subject to debate every time a new federal budget comes to a vote or a major presidential initiative gets introduced on Capitol Hill. When you arrive in Congress, you get a chance to take part in that ongoing debate and in our great experiment with democracy.

Quite simply, members feel the job is satisfying because they are contributing to the direction and the success of this country. They come from all parts of the country and all walks of life, at different stages of their careers, and they seem to disagree on just about everything. Yet almost all would say that by serving in Congress they can make a difference in the lives of people and in the affairs of the nation. They have a commitment to public service and they want to do good—to help their constituencies, their states, and their country as each of them sees fit. There is a certain camaraderie among them, even if they're ideological opponents, that stems from their engagement in the common pursuit of making this a better country. "I have a zeal in my heart, for my country and her friends, which I cannot smother or conceal," John Adams wrote his wife as he headed off to Philadelphia. I don't think that has changed in the 230 years since he wrote those words, either.

4

Public Criticisms of Congress

MANY AMERICANS might go along with my general explanation of how Congress works but still feel that it doesn't work particularly well. Public approval of how Congress is handling its job has typically been very low in recent decades, usually hovering around a 40 percent approval rating—sometimes going higher, sometimes falling below 30 percent.

I heard numerous criticisms of Congress while serving, often in fairly blunt terms. Many of the criticisms seemed to be quite perceptive; others were fairly far off the mark—such as when people thought that as a member of Congress I received a limousine and chauffeur, or enjoyed free medical care, or didn't pay Social Security or income taxes. Even though the attacks were sometimes unpleasant, I always felt it was important for constituents to relay their complaints about Congress, and I never took them lightly. When people are upset about Congress, it undermines public confidence in government and fosters cynicism and disengagement. In a representative democracy like ours, in which Congress must reflect the views and interests of the American people as it frames the basic laws of the land, it really does matter what people think about Congress.

This chapter will sort through several of the main public criticisms of Congress and how it works.

"Legislators Are a Bunch of Crooks"

Several years ago, I was watching the evening news on television when the anchorman announced the death of Wilbur Mills, the legendary former chairman of the House Ways and Means Committee. There was a lot he could have said. He might have recounted the central role Mills had played in creating Medicare. Or he might have talked about how Mills helped to shape the Social Security system and draft the tax code. But he didn't. Instead, he recalled how Mills's career had foundered after he had been found early one morning with an Argentinean stripper named Fanne Foxe. And then he moved on to the next story.

One of the perks of being chairman of an influential committee in Congress, as I was at the time, is that you can pick up the telephone and get through to television news anchors. Which I did: I chided him for summing up the man's career with a scandal. Much to my surprise, he apologized.

The fact is, though, he wasn't doing anything unusual. Americans of all stripes like to dwell on misbehavior by members of Congress. We look at the latest scandal and assume that we're seeing the *real* Congress. But we're not. People might hear repeatedly in the media about missteps, but they hear very little about the House leader who went home on weekends to pastor his local church, or the congressman who devoted decades to championing the needs of the elderly, or the senator who spent one day each month working in a local job to better understand the needs of constituents, or the many members who worked behind the scenes in a bipartisan way to reach the delicate compromises needed to make the system work.

Nor do I see members of Congress as basically out to enrich themselves at the public trough. During my time in office—when I heard numerous complaints about congressional "pay-grabs"—the salaries of members didn't even keep up with inflation. The pay I received in my last year in Congress was $20,000 *less* than if my 1965 pay had been adjusted for inflation. For most members, it is not the money that attracts them to public service; most could be making more in the private sector.

I don't want to claim that all members are saints and that their behavior is impeccable. Improper conduct does occur. Yet I agree with the assessment of historian David McCullough: "Congress, for all its faults, has not been the unbroken parade of clowns and thieves and posturing windbags so often portrayed. What should be spoken of more often, and more widely understood, are the great victories that have been won here, the decisions of courage and vision achieved."[1]

Probity in Congress is the rule rather than the exception, and most experts on Congress agree that it has gotten better over the years. A personal example: Back in the early 1970s, I made an argument in a committee hearing one day favoring military aid for one of our allies. When I got back to my office, I discovered a delegation from that country waiting for me; they wanted to thank me with a fat honorarium, a trip to their country, and an honorary degree from one of their universities. I declined.

The point here isn't my purity. It's that at the time this happened, there was nothing improper about their offer. Today, there would be. When I arrived in Congress, members could accept lavish gifts from special interests, pocket campaign contributions in their Capitol offices, and convert their campaign contributions to personal use. And they were rarely punished for personal corruption. None of that would be tolerated now.

Things still aren't perfect, and I'll return in the next chapter to the need for maintaining and enforcing tough standards of congressional ethics. But the ethical climate at the Capitol is well ahead of where it was a couple of decades ago. And, I might add, it is well ahead of the public perception. From my experience in Congress, getting to know hundreds of members of Congress well over the years, my clear impression is that the vast majority would whole-heartedly agree with Representative Barbara Jordan: "It is a privilege to serve people, a privilege that must be earned, and once earned, there is an obligation to do something good with it."[2]

"There's Too Much Wasteful, Pork-Barrel Spending by Congress"

Some years back, I was at a public meeting in Tell City, Indiana, when one of its citizens stood up to take me and my colleagues to task for our devotion to pork-barrel spending. How in good conscience, he wanted to know, could we spend so much of the public's money on frivolous projects designed only to get us reelected?

My first instinct was to ask him to step outside—but not in the way you might think. To understand why, you have to know a little about Tell City. It is a small town in southern Indiana, founded by Swiss settlers, not far from where Abraham Lincoln ran a ferry across the mouth of the Anderson River as a young man. What you notice in Tell City, though, is a much bigger river, the Ohio, which runs along the edge of its downtown. Indeed, between the building I was standing in and thousands of cubic feet of water lay only a few yards of ground and a levee. And the levee, as you've probably guessed, was built with federal money. If it weren't for this "pork-barrel" project, a good bit of Tell City would long since have been swept away. Pork, I told my audience, is in the eye of the beholder.

The vast majority of federal spending, I would argue, goes to important, widely supported uses. After all, more than half of total federal spending each year goes just for two things—national defense and seniors programs, both very popular. Yet I would agree that you can find some mighty debatable appropriations in each year's federal budget—$1.5 million aimed at refurbishing a statue in one powerful senator's state, $650,000 for ornamental fish research, $90,000 for the National Cowgirl Museum and Hall of Fame, and millions for various memorials and special projects that, in the scheme of things, will benefit relatively few Americans. Congress never fails to provide plenty of material for groups that make it their business to uncover questionable spending.

But think for a moment about what we characterize as "pork-barrel spending." Much of it is for infrastructure: highways, canals, reservoirs, dams, and the like. There's money for erosion-control projects, federal buildings, and military installations. There's support for museums and arts centers. There's backing for academic institutions, health-care facilities, and job-training institutes. All of these have some value and indeed may prove important to lots of people. When it comes to infrastructure spending, "pork-barrel projects" are rarely worthless. Members of Congress know in considerable detail the needs of their district or state, often better than the unelected federal bureaucrat who would otherwise decide where the money goes. We shouldn't fall into the trap of thinking that simply because a senator or representative directs the money to a specific project, it's waste, whereas if a bureaucrat or even the president does, it's not.

At the same time, my scolder in Tell City was on to something. While "pork" may provide valuable support to worthy projects, it can also shore up projects that most of the country would rightly question. The problem is, Congress often doesn't do a good job of distinguishing between the two.

To begin with, pork-barrel projects are frequently inserted by powerful members in spending bills surreptitiously, literally in the dark of night. It may happen within a day of the final vote on a spending measure, and most legislators don't even notice. Nothing is more frustrating for members than to vote for major national legislation only to discover later that it also contained obscure pork-barrel items like a Lawrence Welk memorial. And when legislators do notice a particular project and have concerns about it, they are often reluctant to object, because they may have legislation or projects of their own they don't want to put at risk.

The current process frequently doesn't allow Congress to weigh the relative merit of spending projects, to look at the interests of the country as a whole, or to weigh the needs of one region against another before deciding how to spend the public's money. The problem is not so much that the spending is wasted (it usually does some good) but whether it could better be spent for other projects. Congress often ignores this question and simply provides the money at the request of a member who is powerful or whose vote is badly needed.

We do need to recognize, as I discussed in chapter 2, that much of what Congress passes has an important impact on our lives. But we also need to focus more on wasteful spending, going after the bad apples that get all the attention. A few years ago when I was still in Congress, a reform committee I headed up recommended requiring that no bill could be voted on until all of the funding it earmarked for individual projects was listed clearly in publicly available reports. That would force proponents to justify publicly their provisions for special projects and would help ensure that fewer wasteful projects will pass. Sunshine is still the best disinfectant for wasteful proposals. And on that, I think my critic from Tell City and I could both agree.

"Legislators Just Bicker and Never Get Anything Done"

One of the most common criticisms of Congress is that members spend too much time arguing. I must have heard it a thousand times: Why can't you folks get together?

Congress is generally perceived as the "broken branch" of government, unable to work together to carry out the nation's wishes. Sometimes the language during debates gets a little rough, such as when a member in 1875 described another as "one who is outlawed in his own home from respectable society; whose name is synonymous with falsehood; who is the champion, and has been on all occasions, of fraud; who is the apologist of thieves; who is such a prodigy of vice and meanness that to describe him would sicken imagination and exhaust invective."[3] These comments make the recent partisan squabbling almost sound mild.

The perception of Congress as paralyzed by its own internal bickering comes up in most discussions of the institution, and it is one that matters. Surveys show it is a major factor in the American public's lack of confidence in Congress.

People get upset because they think that everyone agrees on what's right and necessary, and they can't understand why Congress doesn't simply implement the consensus. Yet the truth is that there is far less consensus in the country than is often thought. It is very difficult to get agreement among a broad cross-section of Americans on current major political issues. Most years there is little agreement on what the main issues are, let alone on what specific steps should be taken to address them. The devil—and the dispute—is often in the details.

Most bills passed by Congress actually receive fairly broad, bipartisan support. Yet dispute and delay often occur because it's a tough and tedious job making federal policy. The issues before Congress are much more numerous than in past years, often very complicated and technical, and intensely debated, with a large number of sophisticated groups knowing that key policies and millions of dollars can hinge on every word or comma. The great variety of our nation's races, religions, regional interests, and political philosophies all bring their often-conflicting views to Congress. It's the job of the House and Senate to hear all sides and to search for a broadly acceptable consensus.

There is bound to be bickering when you bring together 535 duly elected representatives and senators—all of whom feel strongly about issues, all of whom want to represent the best interests of their constituents. People shouldn't fall off their chairs because they see heated debate; that's how we thrash things out in a democratic society.

Much of what the public dislikes is part of the process. We could have chosen to have all decisions made by a single ruler at the top, but that's not the kind of government we wanted. Congress was set up as the forum in which strongly held differences would be aired; conflict is built into the system. Allowing all sides a chance to be heard on the most difficult issues facing our nation almost ensures that the debate will at times be contentious, but it also helps to keep our country from ripping apart.

Dispute is different from dysfunction, and results are what count. Intense debate doesn't mean that issues cannot be resolved. It's just that resolving them can be frustrating and time-consuming. I remember many conversations with disgruntled constituents over the years when I urged patience and suggested that they judge Congress by the final results, not by the bickering they might see during the process.

I'm not defending strongly partisan or harsh personal attacks. Certainly things can sometimes go too far and get out of hand. And Congress does have various means for handling such cases—the member in 1875 was in fact formally censured by the House for his remarks. But overall, people should expect some bickering and arguing within Congress. A democracy without conflict is not a democracy.

"You Can't Trust What Members of Congress Say"

I've been looking over some recent survey results on public attitudes toward members of Congress, and I'm worried. People generally give their representatives high marks for being informed about the issues and quite strong approval for their hard work. In fact, three out of four believe that most members of Congress work hard at their jobs. Yet there's an even higher proportion—almost 90 percent—who agree with the statement that most members of Congress will lie if they feel the truth might hurt them politically. That's a lot of Americans who don't trust their elected representatives.

What's interesting to me is that the level of trust *within* Congress—that is, among the senators and representatives who work together day in and day out—is far higher. That is because on Capitol Hill, trust is the coin of the realm; pretty much the worst thing that can happen to a member of Congress is to have word get around among your colleagues that you cannot be relied upon. In order to do their jobs, legislators have to work with others: They cut deals; they agree to support an ally on one issue in exchange for support on something more urgent to their own constituents; they rely on one another to move legislation forward or to block a bill they oppose. Members who renege on their commitments soon find it difficult, if not impossible, to achieve much of what they want—which may explain why I found the overwhelming majority of the hundreds of members of Congress I worked with to be fundamentally honest. I would be hard-pressed to come up with more than a few instances over thirty-four years when I thought fellow members lied to me.

Of course, my relationship with them was as legislator to legislator, not voter to politician. And the truth is, you can understand why there might be a wider gulf between the public and their representatives: Politicians make many speeches; they issue public statements; they give countless media interviews; they respond to letters and inquiries; they hold forums and meetings; they meet constituents in cafés and VFW halls. It's hardly surprising that in the course of this, they would sometimes be inconsistent or even contradictory. But I don't think a blanket criticism that you can't trust members of Congress is fair. So how does one explain it?

To begin with, I think part of the fault lies with members of Congress themselves. They are usually quite skillful with the use of language and parse their words carefully; after all, they want your support and do not want to antagonize you. A politician can often find a way to glide over his or her precise beliefs without actually lying. So it's crucial for members of the public to listen very carefully and ask hard follow-up questions if they find too much wiggle room in an answer.

But it's also true that what might appear to be an inconsistency or a lie is just the result of an honest politician struggling with the complexities of public policy as it moves through different stages of development. For one thing, the circumstances under which a legislator commits to a certain position often change. Think about national security, for instance: The answers our political leaders were giving to questions on security issues on September 10, 2001, were probably very different from the ones they have given since then. By the same token, legislation can take months, if not years, to work its way through the process, and quite often it looks very different at the end from how it started out. So a legislator may initially support a particular bill and tell his or her constituents, but eventually vote against it because amendments in committee or on the floor have made it unpalatable. Votes are, in the end, a blunt instrument: They're yes or no, up or down, and they simply cannot reflect all the nuances of a member's thinking or the changes and complexity of the issues.

It's important to keep this in mind, because on any given issue, a legislator's opinions are usually quite complex, formed through conversations with lobbyists, other legislators, constituents, experts in the field, and others. It is often hard to convey all the nuances, conditions, and qualifications that make up one's position, and even if a politician does so, voters often forget them. Certainly, I've had the experience of a constituent assuring me that I said such-and-such a year ago, when I knew quite well that what I had said was more qualified than that.

I don't want to say that members of Congress never lie. But they do try to be careful with their public statements. They realize that there are a lot of people out there—political opponents, watchdog groups, reporters—who might like to catch them lying or making inconsistent statements. As former Illinois senator Everett Dirksen, known for his flowery oratory, would say, "I must use beautiful words. . . . I never know when I'll have to eat them."[4]

Perhaps Americans' cynicism about their representatives' truthfulness is just part and parcel of living in an age when public service as a whole is looked upon skeptically. Perhaps it's just a broad-brush criticism of Congress, without much to back it up, and people for the most part trust their own particular representative; certainly, the high rate at which members of Congress win reelection suggests they enjoy the support of their constituents. But even if it's simply the institution as a whole that suffers from such extensive distrust, it's a serious problem for representative democracy. And all of us—politicians and voters alike—need to work harder at improving the public dialogue.

"Congress Almost Seems Designed to Promote Total Gridlock"

People will often complain about a "do-nothing" Congress and think much of the fault lies in the basic design of Congress. When a single senator can hold up action on a popular measure, when thirty committees or subcommittees are all reviewing the same bill, when a proposal needs to move not just through both the House and Senate but also through their multilayered budget, authorization, and appropriations processes, when floor procedures are so complex that even members serving several years can still be confused by them—how can you expect to get anything done?

This feeling is magnified by the major changes American society has undergone in recent decades. The incredible increase in the speed of every facet of our lives from communication to transportation, has made many people feel that the slow, untidy, deliberate pace of Congress is not up to the demands of modern society.

It is not now, nor has it ever been, easy to pass legislation through Congress. But there is actually a method to the madness, and basic roadblocks were put into the process for a reason. We live in a great big complicated country, with enormous regional, ethnic, and economic diversity; it is, quite simply, a difficult country to govern. Moving slowly is required for responsiveness and deliberation.

The quest for consensus within Congress can be painfully slow. Issues involving spending and taxes, health care, and access to guns and abortion stir strong emotions and don't submit easily to compromise. Inside-the-Beltway scuffling annoys many Americans, but think about it: Do we really want a speedy system in which laws would be pushed through before a consensus develops? Do we really want a system in which the viewpoint of the minority gets trampled by a rush to action by the majority? Certainly reforms can be made to improve the system, but the basic process of careful deliberation, negotiation, and compromise lies at the very heart of representative democracy. Ours is not a parliamentary system; the dawdling pace comes with the territory.

We misunderstand Congress's role if we demand that it be a model of efficiency and quick action. Our country's founders never intended it to be. They clearly understood that one of the key roles of Congress is to slow down the process—to allow tempers to cool and to encourage careful deliberation, so that unwise or damaging laws do not pass in the heat of the moment and so that the views of those in the minority get a fair hearing. That basic vision still seems wise today. Proceeding carefully to develop consensus is arduous and exasperating, but it's the only way to produce policies that reflect the varied perspectives of a remarkably diverse citizenry. People may complain about the process, yet they also benefit from its legislative speed bumps when they want their views heard, their interests protected, their rights safeguarded. As Sam Rayburn used to say: "One of the wisest things ever said was, 'Wait a minute.'"

I'll return to this topic in the next chapter, discussing what sorts of reforms could make Congress work better. I certainly recognize that sometimes there are too many roadblocks in the system and Congress needlessly gets bogged down. Some streamlining and institutional reform is often needed, and I've been involved in many of those reform efforts. Yet I still believe that the fundamental notion that the structure of Congress should contain roadblocks and barriers to hasty action and unfair action makes sense for our country and needs to be protected and preserved.

"Members of Congress Compromise Too Much"

Every two years while I served in Congress, almost like clockwork, I'd open my mail to find the questionnaire. When you run for office, you expect various organizations to examine your positions on the issues they care about, but the group that sent this one out always went to greater lengths than most. For page after page, they'd ask me yes or no questions about matters large and small. There was no room for shades of gray; in their eyes, policy decisions were a matter of black or white.

I always felt boxed into a corner by this, even though I sympathized with their effort to publicize candidates' positions. If you take a larger view of the legislative process, they were doing themselves—and the rest of us—a disservice. At its best, politics is not a matter of holding onto your opinions no matter what; it's the art of finding common ground with people who think differently, then forging a workable approach to resolving a problem. This usually involves a compromise. Groups interested only in locking legislators into a rigid position make it more difficult for our democracy to work.

To be sure, many Americans don't understand this. Surveys show that three out of five believe that "compromise" means selling out one's principles and that members of Congress compromise too much. But think for a moment about what this means. What are the options when you can't forge a compromise? If the forces interested in the matter are equally strong, you get an impasse: Nothing happens. If they're not evenly matched, you get a triumphant majority and a deeply unhappy minority—a situation our nation's founders repeatedly warned against. And in the worst case, which our nation experienced when it came to the institution of slavery, you get a civil war.

At the end of the day, the responsibility of our politicians is to make the country work, to provide stability and an environment in which Americans can live in freedom and achieve their goals. In a nation as big and diverse as ours, in which so many people hold so many differing opinions, that means finding solutions to issues that allow us to work peaceably and productively together; and that, in turn, means finding compromises. It is what our founders did when they wrote the Constitution—they compromised on everything, from how small and large states would be represented to their deferment of the issue of slavery—and it is what virtually every piece of major legislation passed by Congress has required. As former House Speaker Joseph Cannon often said, "Nearly all legislation is the result of compromise."[5]

There are, of course, members of Congress who promise in their election campaigns to "fight for" their constituents, or for a particular cause, without backing down. But they usually discover that it is very difficult to be effective in Congress unless they learn how to build consensus. For the bottom line is, you cannot pass legislation unless you can get 218 members of the House of Representatives and 51 members of the Senate (frequently more) to agree with you. Members who don't learn the art of compromise usually find themselves on the margins of the legislative process. At the same time, every member of Congress has certain core beliefs on which he or she will not compromise; as much as finding common ground is part of the art of legislating, so, too, is weighing whether or not one is giving up too much in order to move an issue forward. Legislators make tough calls like that every day.

I don't wish to diminish those legislators who are deeply committed to an issue and choose to stick to it even at the risk of appearing to be a gadfly. They too serve our democracy, because these sometimes lone voices may, over time, change the agenda, shift the emphasis on an issue, or influence the nature of the resulting compromise. But if all legislators shunned consensus in favor of single-minded devotion to a cause, nothing would get done.

It has grown more difficult in recent years to practice the politics of consensus. This is due partly to the rising partisanship that has marked Congress over the past dozen years or so, partly to a press corps that always wants an immediate response and is ready to pounce on any instance of "inconsistency" in a politician's position, partly to the openness with which much of the legislative process operates these days, and partly to voters and interest groups who demand "purity" in a legislator's positions. Don't get me wrong: I think much good has come out of opening committees and other venues for deliberation to allow the public to see their representatives in action, and I supported many congressional "sunshine" reforms over the years. But I also think that legislators need room to act like politicians, to search for broadly acceptable solutions to difficult problems.

For one of the keenest insights our founders possessed was that the process by which we arrive at decisions matters a great deal. Legislating is not like war, in which one side strives to impose its will on the other. It is, rather, a shared path, the route we all must follow as we try to live with one another and struggle together to resolve the difficult questions that always confront us. We want our legislators to be able to work together, to give some ground when they need to in order to move forward. "If every compromise is taken as a defeat that must be overturned," wrote the eminent American historian Bernard Bailyn not long ago, "and if no healing generosity is shown to defeated rivals, the best-contrived constitution in the world would not succeed."[6] A willingness to compromise is nothing more or less than the recognition that we're all in this together for the long haul and that each of us has a stake in the system by which we govern ourselves.

"There's Too Much Money in Politics Today"

People hear the stories about all the fund-raising that members must do today, and so they believe that Congress is a "bought" institution. Often they would tell me that in our system dollars speak louder than words and that access is bought and sold. By a four-to-one margin, Americans believe that elected officials are influenced more by pressures from campaign contributors than by what is in the best interests of the country.

The problem of money in politics has been with us for many years. But it has really emerged as a serious problem in recent decades with the advent of television advertising. The biggest portion of my $1 million campaign budget—for a largely rural seat in southern Indiana—went for television.

Having experienced it firsthand, it is clear to me that the "money chase" has gotten out of hand. A lot of money from special interests is floating around Capitol Hill—in fact, far too much money. I believe it's a problem we ignore at our own peril.

To be fair, many of the claims of special interests buying influence in Congress are overstated. I would be the last to say that contributions have no impact on a member's voting record. But it should also be kept in mind that most of the money comes from groups who already share your views on the issues and want to see you reelected, rather than from groups who are hoping to change your mind. In addition, many influences shape members' voting decisions—including their assessment of the arguments, the opinions of experts and colleagues, their party's position, and, most importantly, what their constituents want. In the end, members know that if their votes aren't in line with what their constituents want, they simply won't be reelected. And that, rather than a campaign contribution, is what is foremost in their minds.

Yet it is still an unusual member of Congress who can take thousands of dollars from a particular group and not be affected by it at all. I have come to the view that the influence of money on the political process raises a threat to representative democracy. But more on that in the next chapter. Overall, this is an area in which I agree that significant reform is needed. It is also, unfortunately, an area in which there are no easy answers.

"Members Are Out of Touch with Their Constituents"

It always makes me wince when I hear someone criticize Congress as "out of touch" with what the people are thinking. I heard this complaint regularly when I was in Congress. Polls consistently show that more than 60 percent of the public do not expect their elected officials to be responsive to their thoughts.

This is a long-standing problem. Some of America's most animated political debates over the years have focused on whether the federal government is in close enough touch with the concerns of the average citizen. The framers of the Constitution fought at length on this point. One faction, led by Virginia's George Mason, called for many seats in the House of Representatives, so each district would be small enough for "common men" to personally communicate their concerns to House members. They were opposed by the Federalists, who argued that if each member represented more people, the House would more likely act in the national interest.

Under our system of representative democracy, members of Congress are asked not just to pass the nation's laws but also to represent in Washington the interests of the districts and states they represent. This means that staying in touch with constituents remains a fundamental challenge. It isn't a problem that will soon be going away.

I know how difficult it is for members of Congress to keep in touch with their huge constituencies. Some congressional districts are geographically vast—a single House member, for example, represents all of Alaska—and the population of each of our 435 House districts now averages 650,000 people, a number the founders could scarcely have imagined. When the first Congress convened in 1789, each of its sixty-five House members represented around 30,000 people. Our congressional constituencies today are the largest in the world, except for those in India.

The way Congress was set up, the House is assigned primary responsibility for understanding and voicing the concerns of the people. That's why the Constitution mandates House elections every two years. If the House fails in its job as chief citizen-advocate, then the people's faith in the federal government is eroded.

Contrary to the public perception, most legislators try very hard to keep in touch. They understand their weighty responsibility and think about this all the time. It is a constant topic of conversation among members over lunch or as they walk together between meetings—always comparing techniques, always trying to find ways to improve their outreach to constituents.

Indeed, I think a case could be made that the opposite may in fact be closer to the truth—that members today might be paying *too much* attention to every blip in the public opinion polls, thinking *too much* about what would play well back in the district, rather than focusing on what would be good policy and good for the country. So a balance is needed.

Members employ a wide variety of methods to reach out to constituents—traditional ones like sending out newsletters, hosting local forums, encouraging office visits, participating in radio and television call-in shows, and attending civic functions and community festivals, as well as using the latest technology for satellite hookups, video conferencing, and "virtual town meetings" over the Internet. They make sure that constituents who write, e-mail, fax, or contact their congressman get a letter in response.

Because House districts now are so populous, even a frenetic pace allows a member to reach only a small portion of his or her constituency. And yet members keep trying to push the envelope on public contact, particularly when they are back home. They do this because handshaking at the county fair and Fourth of July parades and other such gatherings is often the only way to have any contact with constituents who are indifferent to politics or are simply too busy in their everyday lives to bother to write or call their congressman.

Most members of Congress feel a deep sense of obligation to reach out to the public. It is an ongoing challenge for them, and they recognize they simply need to keep working at it.

Legislators have been struggling at this for more than two hundred years without resolving it. Citizens, too, need to understand their obligation to make our democratic system function well. They have some responsibility to help their representative *not* get out of touch by initiating contacts and responding when they can to members' outreach efforts. It takes the participation and goodwill of all to make our system work.

"Congress Is Run by Lobbyists and Special Interests"

Americans have different views of lobbyists and special interests. Some see them as playing an essential part in the democratic process. Others look at them with some skepticism, but understand that they have a role to play in developing policy. Yet most see them as sinister forces with too much control of Congress. The recent Enron and Arthur Andersen scandals, and revelations about those companies' extensive lobbying of Congress, have fed this cynicism about the hold that powerful private interests maintain over public policy. Americans continue to remain suspicious that Congress is manipulated by powerful wheeler-dealers who put enormous pressure on legislators or buy votes through extensive campaign contributions and other favors. It is not an unfounded concern, and it is not going to go away, no matter how fervently some might try to dismiss it.

Now, the popular view of lobbyists as nefarious fat cats smoking big cigars and handing out $100 bills behind closed doors is wrong. These days, lobbyists are usually principled people who recognize that their word is their bond. They are aggressive in seeking out members of Congress, offering to take them to dinner for a chance at a longer conversation, and operating from a carefully worked-out game plan that takes into account who might be persuaded to vote their way, when they ought to be approached, and whether they have interested constituents who can be used effectively to put pressure on them. Lobbying is an enormous industry today with billions of dollars riding on its outcomes. Special interest groups will often spend millions of dollars on campaigns to influence a particular decision—through political contributions, grassroots lobbying efforts, television advocacy ads, and the like—because they know they can get a lot more back than they spent. Lobbyists who can get the kind of language they want into a bill can reap very large rewards. They are very good at what they do, and members of Congress can sometimes be easily swayed by them.

The influence of lobbyists on the process is not as simple as it might appear. In the first place, "special interests" are not just the bad guys. If you're retired, or a homeowner, or use public transit, or fly on airplanes, or are concerned about religious freedom, there are people in Washington lobbying on your behalf. With an estimated 25,000 interest groups lobbying in Washington, you can be sure your views are represented in many ways. Advocacy groups help Congress understand how legislation affects their members, and they help focus the public's attention on important issues. They play a vital role in amplifying the flow of information that Thomas Jefferson called the "dialogue of democracy."

In addition, Congress often takes up controversial, attention-grabbing issues on which you'll find an entire spectrum of opinions. Public notice is high, a host of special interests are weighing in, and lobbyists as well as legislators themselves are all over the map. In these circumstances, the prospect is very small that any single interest group or lobbyist can disproportionately influence the results. Quite simply, there are too many of them involved for that to happen, and the process is too public.

Where you have to look out is when things get quiet, when measures come up that are out of the public eye. A small change in wording here, an innocuous line in a tax bill there—that's where specific groups can reap enormous benefits that might not have been granted had they been held up to close public scrutiny.

The answer, it seems to me, is not to decry lobbying or lobbyists. In our system of government, we make a lot of trade-offs, as James Madison warned more than two centuries ago when he argued that "factions" were part of the cost of maintaining a democracy. At heart, lobbying is simply people banding together to advance their interests, whether they are farmers or environmentalists or bankers. Belonging to an interest group—the Sierra Club, the AARP, the Chamber of Commerce—is one of the main ways Americans participate in public life these days.

When I was in Congress, I found that organized groups not only brought a useful perspective to the table. They also pointed out how a given measure might affect my constituents in ways I hadn't considered. Lobbyists are typically professionals with a variety of skills: They are experts in their subject, with a sophisticated knowledge of the political process and the ability to raise large sums of money and make campaign contributions. They maintain extensive contacts, can generate grassroots support, and often have experience in putting together winning coalitions. I came to think of lobbyists as an important part of the *public discussion* of policy.

I emphasize "public discussion" for a reason. Sunshine is a powerful disinfectant, and rather than trying to clamp down on lobbying, I believe we would be better off ensuring that it happens in the open and is part of the broader policy debate.

So our challenge is not to shut it down but to make sure it's a balanced dialogue and that those in power don't consistently listen to the voices of the wealthy and the powerful more intently than to others. Several legislative proposals have been made over the years that would help, including campaign finance reform, strict limits on gifts to members of Congress, travel restrictions for members and their staffs funded by groups with a direct interest in legislation, and effective disclosure of the role lobbyists play in drafting legislation. But in the end, something may be even more important: ongoing conversation between elected officials and the people they represent.

Under our system of government, there is absolutely nothing wrong with lobbyists advocating their point of view. Lobbying is a key element of the legislative process and part of the free speech guaranteed under our Constitution. Members of Congress, I would argue, have a responsibility to listen to lobbyists. But members also have a responsibility to understand where these lobbyists are coming from, to sort through what they are saying, and then to make a judgment about what is in the best interests of their constituents and the nation as a whole.

Conclusion

Members of Congress most often will hear from constituents on specific policy issues—how the legislator should vote, issues that need more attention, local problems that aren't being addressed. But equally important is hearing complaints about how Congress as an institution is working. If people are upset that members seem increasingly dishonest or out of touch, that special interests seem to be taking over, or that there is too much partisan bickering or legislative gridlock or whatever—all of these are important things for members of Congress to hear.

Such feedback is essential for keeping Congress on course. It's how Congress adjusts itself when it gets off track—hearing from all corners that something is just not right and then trying to be responsive. Making Congress work better is not just a matter for the political scientists or the political commentators or the legislators themselves. Congress really is the people's branch, and we all have the responsibility to keep an eye on it and to speak up when we're bothered by what we see. It's an essential part of the ongoing dialogue of democracy.

5

Key Ways Congress Could Work Better

AMERICANS CLEARLY HAVE DEEP CONCERNS about Congress, but they wouldn't want to abandon their long-established form of government. In all the years I was in Congress, although my constituents were not at all hesitant about bashing Congress, they still thought it important for it to be around.

There is, in short, strong support for the institution of the Congress—for its role in the balance of powers, for its role in giving a voice to the people, for its role as a forum for resolving national differences—but also deep frustration with its operations and day-to-day functioning, a frustration, I might add, often shared by many members.

So how do we make Congress work better—restoring greater confidence in its operations and making it a more effective, less frustrating body? Given the way it was set up under the Constitution, with numerous checks and balances and multiple layers to allow all voices a chance to be heard, Congress will never be a model of efficiency. Yet important improvements can still be made. This chapter contains several basic changes that I believe are central to the proper functioning of Congress. Rather than presenting a long list of technical changes in the legislative and budget processes, I've focused on broader, more fundamental improvements, a few suggestions from the perspective of someone who has spent more than three decades immersed in this fascinating, complex institution.

Declining Civility

Not long ago I was asked to give a talk on how Congress has changed since 1965, the year I entered it as a young freshman member from southern Indiana. As I sat looking through my old speeches, a phrase jumped out at me. Congress, I told my audiences back then, did its work in an "extraordinarily hospitable atmosphere." Indeed, I liked to say, no matter how spirited the policy debate, "a cocoon of warmth" surrounded us.

If I suggested anything of the sort today I'd be laughed out of the room. The last several years have been particularly divisive and partisan. Certainly tough times in Congress are nothing new—going back even to the Second Congress, in 1791, when partisan differences undermined its ability to function, and including the memorable floor debate in the 1850s when thirty members pulled their guns. Yet, during my time in Congress, I witnessed a marked change in its atmosphere: the demonization of people in the other party, nasty personal attacks, a willingness to pull out all the stops to undermine the other side's agenda, and concerted efforts to topple the other party's leader.

Breakdowns in civility are among the most serious threats to the ability of Congress to work well. Spirited, even heated debates and aggressively pushing the interests of your constituents are to be expected and are healthy to the institution. That's how issues get thrashed out in a democratic society. But personal attacks and excessive partisanship poison the atmosphere of Congress and undermine the ability of members to come together to do the nation's business. It even got so bad in the 1990s that Representative John

Myers, a Republican colleague from Indiana, and I requested a report from the Congressional Research Service on the rules and precedents governing civility and decorum in the House and circulated it to all of our colleagues.

Yet the situation isn't hopeless. Some periods are distressing, yet others do give reason for hope. In 1995, one of my last years in Congress, there was a stark ideological divide between Democrats and the Republican majority. Debates were contentious and bitterly uncompromising; legislators almost came to blows on a few occasions. As the country watched with increasing disapproval, the congressional leadership that winter shut down much of the federal government for twenty-seven days, a move that caused Congress's standing with the public to plummet.

Then something important happened. Just before the traditional August break in 1996, Congress turned itself around. In the space of just ten days, Democrats and Republicans came together and passed several major bills—overhauling the federal welfare program, expanding access to health insurance, increasing the minimum wage, and rewriting safe drinking water legislation. Congress showed very quickly and very clearly that even when it appears ready to sink, it can right itself. Faced with the prospect of returning to their districts not only empty-handed but widely reviled for their obstinate partisanship, members of Congress rediscovered pragmatism. They sat down together and wrote laws.

Congress is a partisan body, but it is also a responsive body. When constituents are tired of division and blatant partisan calculation, members of Congress hear about it when they go home, and they change course. The surprise would be if members *did not* pay attention. It is Congress's own self-correcting mechanism at work.

I don't want to overstate the point. The basic forces that over the years have produced this partisan era are not simply going to fade away: the rise of personal attack campaigns and their frequent success, the intense pressure on members' time that leaves little opportunity to develop friendships across the aisle, the hard-fought battle for that. For more than two centuries Congress has preserved free government and prevented tyranny. It is still the protector of our freedom and the premier forum for addressing the key issues of the day and connecting our voices to the counsels of power. All of us need to look at Congress realistically, critically, even skeptically. But we also need to view it at times with a sense of gratitude and a sense that it has mattered. It not only makes a difference in our lives. It also helps us make a difference in the lives of others.

Our great experiment in representative democracy has served us well, but it fundamentally rests upon informed citizens who understand the essential nature of our system and participate in our civic life. That is how Congress truly works.

Appendix

Communicating with Congress

There are many ways for citizens to communicate with their members of Congress: phone, mail, fax, e-mail, or in person. Here are some sources to help you identify and then connect with your House representative or your senators.

Identifying Your Members of Congress

Find your Senators: http://www.senate.gov
Find your House Representative: http://www.house.gov

Making Contact by Phone

Senate switchboard: 202-224-3121
House switchboard: 202-225-3121

Making Contact by Mail

Write to any member of the Senate at this address:
    The Honorable (full name)
    U.S. Senate
    Washington, DC 20510
Write to any member of the House at this address:
    The Honorable (full name)
    U.S. House of Representatives
    Washington, DC 20515

Making Contact by E-mail

For the Senate: http://www.senate.gov/contacting/index.cfm
For the House: http://www.house.gov/writerep/wyrfaqs.htm#listrep

Making Contact in Person

Members of Congress have offices both in Washington, D.C., and in their state/ district. To schedule an appointment or to learn times of local public meetings, call or e-mail.

Communication Tips:

1. State the purpose of your contact clearly. If commenting on a specific piece of legislation, give its bill number.
2. Be brief.
3. Lawmakers understand that people are often upset, but try to be courteous.
4. Use your own words to explain how the issue affects you or your family personally.
5. Be as accurate as possible. Getting your facts straight is essential.
6. Keep in mind that members of Congress really do want to hear your views.

Notes

1. The Role of Congress

1. James Madison, *The Federalist*, no. 51, February 6, 1788.
2. John Adams, included in *The Founders' Constitution*, ed. Philip B. Kurland and Ralph Lerner (Chicago: University of Chicago Press, 1987), chap. 11, document 16.
3. Bernard Bailyn, *To Begin the World Anew* (New York: Alfred A. Knopf, 2003), p. 4.
4. John Adams, included in *The Founders' Constitution*, chap. 4, document 5.
5. Thomas Jefferson, included in *The Founders' Constitution*, chap. 8, document 44.
6. See James Burnham, *Congress and the American Tradition* (Chicago: Henry Regnery, 1959), p. 98.
7. See Walter J. Oleszek, *Congressional Procedures and the Policy Process*, 4th ed. (Washington, D.C.: CQ Press, 1996), p. 19.
8. James Madison, *The Federalist*, no. 58, February 20, 1788.
9. Both quotations from James H. Hutson, *To Make All Laws: The Congress of the United States, 1789–1989* (Boston: Houghton Mifflin, 1990).
10. Richard Henry Lee, included in *The Founders' Constitution*, chap. 14, document 21.
11. Quoted in Louis Brandeis, quoted in *Government by Judiciary: A Transformation of the Fourteenth Amendment*, 2d ed. (Indianapolis: Liberty Fund, 1997), p. 384.
12. Quoted in Val J. Halamandaris, ed., *Heroes of the U.S. Congress: A Search for the Hundred Greatest Members of Congress* (Washington, D.C.: Caring, 1994), p. 193.

2. The Impact of Congress

1. Halamandaris, *Heroes of the U.S. Congress*, p. 143.
2. See Paul Charles Light, *Government's Greatest Achievements: From Civil Rights to Homeland Defense* (Washington, D.C.: Brookings Institution Press, 2002).

3. How Congress Works

1. Artemus Ward, quoted in *Government in America: People, Politics, and Policy*, 9th ed., ed. George C. Edwards III, Martin P. Wattenberg, and Robert L. Lineberry (New York: Longman, 2000), p. 370.

2. Woodrow Wilson, *Congressional Government,* 2d ed. (Boston: Houghton Mifflin, 1885), p. 69.

3. See Alan Rosenthal, Karl T. Kurtz, John Hibbing, and Burdett Loomis, *The Case for Representative Democracy: What Americans Should Know about Their Legislatures* (Denver: National Conference of State Legislatures, 2001), chap. 3.

4. Quoted in Roger H. Davidson and Walter J. Oleszek, *Congress and Its Members,* 6th ed. (Washington, D.C.: Congressional Quarterly, 1998), p. 8.

5. Quoted in Hutson, *To Make All Laws,* p. 5.

6. John Adams to Abigail Adams, October 9, 1774, Massachusetts Historical Society, Adams Family Archive.

4. Public Criticisms of Congress

1. David McCullough, Bicentennial Address to Congress, March 2, 1989.

2. Halamandaris, *Heroes of the U.S. Congress,* p. 98.

3. Rep. John Young Brown of Kentucky, House floor debate, February 4, 1875.

4. Halamandaris, *Heroes of the U.S. Congress,* p. 42.

5. Ibid., p. 26.

6. Bailyn, *To Begin the World Anew,* p. 124.

5. Key Ways Congress Could Work Better

1. See Lee H. Hamilton, with Jordan Tama, *A Creative Tension: The Foreign Policy Roles of the President and Congress* (Washington, D.C.: Woodrow Wilson Center Press, 2002).

2. Wilson, *Congressional Government,* p. 195.

3. Hubert H. Humphrey quoted in David W. Adamany and George E. Agree, *Political Money: A Strategy for Campaign Financing in America* (Baltimore: Johns Hopkins University Press, 1975), p. 8.

4. See Hutson, *To Make All Laws,* p. 25.

5. See John R. Hibbing and Elizabeth Theiss-Morse, *Congress as Public Enemy: Public Attitudes toward American Political Institutions* (New York: Cambridge University Press, 1995), p. 1.

6. Civic Participation

1. Quoted in Thomas E. Patterson, *The American Democracy,* 5th ed. (Boston: McGraw Hill, 2001), p. 184.

2. Quoted in Stephen E. Frantzich, *Citizen Democracy: Political Activists in a Cynical Age* (Lanham, Md.: Rowman and Littlefield, 1999), p. 7.

3. See Michael Schudson, *The Good Citizen: A History of American Civic Life* (Cambridge: Harvard University Press, 1999), p. 311.

4. For these and other examples, see Frantzich, *Citizen Democracy,* and George C. Edwards et al., *Government in America: People, Politics, and Policy.*

5. Quoted in Stanley Elkins and Eric McKitrick, *The Age of Federalism: The Early American Republic, 1788–1800* (New York: Oxford University Press, 1995), p. 75.

6. Halamandaris, *Heroes of the U.S. Congress,* p. 197.

Index

Lee H. Hamilton was U.S. Representative from Indiana's Ninth District from 1965 to 1999. He served as Chairman of the House Committee on Foreign Affairs, the Permanent Select Committee on Intelligence, the Joint Economic Committee, and the Joint Committee on the Organization of Congress, and worked to promote the integrity and efficiency of Congress as an institution. He is now Director of the Woodrow Wilson International Center for Scholars in Washington, D.C., and Director of the Center on Congress at Indiana University.